NATIONALISM, TECHNOLOGY
AND THE FUTURE OF CANADA

Nationalism, Technology and the Future of Canada

EDITED BY
WALLACE GAGNE

Macmillan of Canada
Maclean-Hunter Press

© 1976 The Macmillan Company of Canada Limited

Canadian Cataloguing in Publication Data

Main entry under title:

Nationalism, technology and the future of Canada

Bibliography: p.
ISBN 0-7705-1347-6 bd.   ISBN 0-7705-1348-4 pa.

1. Nationalism—Canada—Addresses, essays, lectures.
2. Technology—Social aspects—Canada—Addresses, essays, lectures. 3. Canada—Economic conditions—1945—   Addresses, essays, lectures. I. Gagne, Wallace, 1943-

FC97.N3   320.5′4′0971   C76-017062-2
F1034.2.N3

Printed in Canada for
The Macmillan Company of Canada Limited
70 Bond Street
Toronto, Ontario
M5B 1X3

CONTENTS

NATIONALISM, TECHNOLOGY
AND THE FUTURE OF CANADA

Introduction

The history of Canada is the history of a country which has never become independent. While we enjoy formal political independence, many of our key economic, political and social decisions are strongly influenced and even controlled by outsiders, particularly the Americans. Ours is a history written in terms of "colonial status," "imperial connection" and "continentalism," rather than "Canadian Revolution," "self-determination" and "national independence." For three centuries we have alternated between occasional futile attempts to become truly independent and long periods when we have failed even to make the attempt, settling instead for cosy understandings with others which have enhanced our prosperity, but done little to serve our long-term interests. While this course may once have served our needs, it is a course which holds great dangers in the future. New forces and new ideas are rapidly becoming dominant throughout the world, which not only threaten the independence of most smaller nations, but the independence and dignity of man himself. Unless we can understand the nature of these dangers and begin working towards alternatives, we will face a future in which Canada ceases to exist and Canadians will face the most profound threats.

While much concern has been expressed about the problem of Canadian independence, there have been few attempts to examine the issue within a sufficiently broad range of economic, political and social forces to permit either a more complete understanding of the issue or the formulation of suitable alternatives. Generally, most scholars have tended to focus rather narrowly on such problems as the amount of foreign ownership of the Canadian economy, the lack of an independent foreign policy, or the degree of outside cultural influence. Similarly, most of those proposing alternatives have relied rather simply on the measures of traditional nationalism to solve these problems, advocating that the federal government protect the Canadian nation through such policies as increasing Canadian ownership, developing an independent foreign policy or imposing Canadian-content quotas.

While this approach is undoubtedly well-intentioned, and serves to address some of the more obvious features of the independence question, it fails to explain why we have become so dependent on others or to relate proposed alternatives to the highly interdependent and technological world which is emerging. By concentrating on the results and ignoring the causes, this approach produces only piecemeal solutions which may offer some short-term protection for Canadian independence, but will do little to meet the economic, political and human dangers of the future.

Another serious difficulty with the traditional nationalist approach is that it ignores much about the basic nature of Canadian politics, particularly the fact that nationalism is directly counter to most of the forces which have shaped the institutions and traditions of our politics. It is important to consider that Canadians have never enjoyed that high degree of internal cohesion which is necessary to be called a nation. We have always found it difficult to implement national policies and have always been suspicious of centralizing concepts such as nationalism. Only in periods of great necessity, such as wartime, have we been able to overcome many of our differences, and even then we could sometimes mount a powerful effort only by imposing embittering measures, such as conscription, on those of our people who disagreed with the necessity. In order to deal with the independence question realistically, it is crucial to appreciate the essentially regional and communal nature of our politics and to formulate alternatives which are relevant to that nature. Without this appreciation, attempts to achieve greater independence through poorly considered centralist policies could well produce even greater dangers than those they are designed to overcome.

If we are to understand the independence question in all its complexity and formulate alternatives which are relevant, then we must begin to contemplate it in new ways. Essentially we must adopt a much more holistic approach by seeing it as part of a whole matrix of relationships among nations, economies and people, which cannot be explained by a single theory or isolated as a single variable. We must go beyond static interpretations of the world, and see ourselves as part of a dynamic whole in which relationships and values are constantly changing, and where traditional beliefs about the nature of man are being replaced by new conceptions of what man is and what he should do.

Another way of expressing this necessity is to say that we must be open to the nature of technique and what it implies for man. This is so because much of what we are, and what we think is the nature of the good, is rooted in technique—that system of values and beliefs which drives man to master nature and exploit it as a resource. More than anything, it was our acceptance of technique and the benefits which flow from it which has spurred Canadians to regard the massive development of our natural resources as a positive good, and to pursue that good regardless of whether we developed these resources ourselves, or through a policy of foreign ownership and control. By accepting technique, we essentially accepted a new set of values in which progress and development are ranked higher than more traditional values such as sovereignty and national independence. If we hope to use political means to develop alternatives to our present course, then we must understand the relationship between our politics and the values of technique. Policies which do not recognize this relationship have little chance of popular acceptance because most Canadians would find them irrelevant to their present way of life. Unless they can be shown what is wrong with the present course and what alternatives are possible, they are likely to continue voicing an interest in the independence question but remain unwilling to sacrifice anything of consequence in order to bring about necessary changes.

In attempting to work for an alternative future, we must also contemplate the growing interdependence between economic and political systems which is taking place throughout the world, and which is making many traditional types of politics obsolete. In previous ages, it was possible, at least in part, to regard the economic and political parts of society as separate phenomena, and to study them accordingly. Now, however, they are so closely tied that it is virtually impossible to analyse any major economic decisions without considering the political factors which are almost always involved at the centre of the decision-making process. Moreover, we must relate our situation to the new and highly integrated system of production which is developing throughout the world if we hope to plan for future contingencies. This new, worldwide interdependence has already undermined many traditional conceptions of independence, and will undoubtedly produce even greater pressures as resource shortages, inflationary crises and population pressures become more severe. Given these developments, it is imperative that we think carefully about what independence could mean in such a dynamic world, why we would want to achieve it, and how we should work to bring it about. If we, and the other industrialized nations, opt merely to retreat into a narrow, isolationist type of nationalism in the face of the present and future difficulties facing the world, then we could all become victims of the same type of forces which shattered world peace during the 1930s.

One of the serious problems we face in developing a more holistic understanding of the independence question is that much of the existing methodology and many of the current theories of the humanities and social sciences are thoroughly inadequate. Many false and arbitrary barriers have been erected within these areas, supposedly for the purpose of specializing knowledge and making research more efficient. The result has been the production of much compartmentalized knowledge and isolated inferences which may meet academic standards but

have all the usefulness of ships in glass bottles. If we are to surmount this difficulty, then we must develop new methods and
theories which not only help us to understand the dynamic
nature of the world which is now unfolding, but also help us to
devise strategies for coming to terms with it.

The task ahead is indeed formidable. No single mind or
single book can even begin to set forth the ideas and relationships which must be understood. Many minds and much
thought are needed to examine the values, assess the structures,
construct the theories and formulate the alternatives. This will
require the cooperation of people in many diverse areas and
with many different types of expertise. Ultimately, however, the
true test of this effort will be how it is synthesized into a coherent body of thought and then, in turn, how this thought is
acted upon.

Even though the issue of Canada's independence may appear
as a miniscule part of what is now developing throughout the
world, we should not regard it in this light. Rather, we should
recognize that the future of Canada and Canadians is equally
as important as the future of any other state or any other people.
All who are serious about humanity must engage in the same
contemplation as we, whether it is within the context of achieving some form of independence, overcoming great social divisions, or simply facing the dangers of the future as individual
beings. Perhaps in our attempt to understand and meet our future, we can provide them with some useful insight or strategy.
The essays brought together in this book are an attempt by a
few Canadians to say something useful about the problem of our
independence and to propose alternatives to our present
course. They should not be taken as a comprehensive discussion of all factors involved in the issue, but as a modest attempt
to begin developing the understanding of the issue which we
so desperately require. The remaining pages of this introduction
briefly describe the essays and show how they relate to the general question of Canada's independence.

In selecting the topics of the essays, two concerns were paramount: the first was to try to develop the type of holistic discussion of the independence question which to date has been
seriously lacking in much of the writing about Canadian nation-

alism; the second was to attempt to re-examine specific aspects of that question within this more holistic context. To that end, the authors of the first three essays have adopted a broad approach to Canadian nationalism, while the other three have focused on more specific concerns, such as our relationship with the United States. It is hoped that the reader will first obtain a fairly pervasive perspective of the independence question and will then be able to understand and evaluate the more specific and practical aspects.

The first two essays are primarily concerned with the relationship between technology and Canadian nationalism. In my work "Technology and Canadian Politics," I rely primarily on the thought of Martin Heidegger to establish the meaning of technology and technique, and then show how our acceptance of technical values has affected the development of our politics, particularly our national independence. In the second part of my essay, I attempt to formulate an alternative to our present state of dependency by examining the communal aspect of our politics and by showing how the concept of community could be used to form the basis of an independent Canada in which local communities work to overcome the dangers of the technological society, as well as the difficulties of outside control.

In the second essay, "Nationalism and Communitarianism in Canada," Howard Aster develops an extensive analysis of the relationship between technology and nationalism, relying on the thought of Francis Bacon to show the nature of the technological perspective. According to Professor Aster, modern nationalism, which is essentially ideological, has developed in concert with modern technology, which is essentially instrumental, to produce the belief that nation-building can be achieved through the utilization of instrumental knowledge. This modern form of nationalism contrasts with the earlier form which was essentially organic and evolutionary. It is Professor Aster's contention that the modern form of liberal nationalism is essentially in conflict with the communitarian nature of Canadian society, and that if Canadians wish to enjoy an independent and creative politics, then they must base their attempts on these communitarian foundations.

In the third essay, John Woods adopts "A Cultural Approach to Canadian Independence." He raises the question of what our independence provides and how these particular benefits are to be preserved. According to Professor Woods, there is a "Canadian Identity" which makes us sufficiently different to warrant our independence, but we must be careful in how we attempt to develop and protect that identity in order to make our independence truly significant. Thus, we must recognize the essentially diverse nature of Canadian society and within that diversity begin to sort out those internal and external influences which can be integrated into our lifestyle, while rejecting those which cannot. If we take the position that "the only acceptable nationalism is that of cultural coherence," then "we should, in the event, let Canada fade away as a focus of our loyalty," since under the circumstances Canada would serve no useful purpose.

Having examined the nationalist question in these broad terms, the next three essays concentrate on more particular aspects of Canada's independence, most of which are external, but some of which are internal. Two critical subjects which demand action before we can begin building an independent and alternative form of society are our relationships with the United States and our reliance on American-dominated trade unions. Unless we can develop a much more independent policy towards the United States and regain control of our key economic structures, there is little chance of implementing those significant changes in our political and social structures which make independence worth having.

In the area of Canadian-American relations, it is now time to think carefully about the nature of our colonial relationship with the United States, and begin developing a new relationship which maintains joint amiability yet affirms our power of self-determination. In "Canadian-American Relations: Anti-Nationalist Myths and Colonial Realities," Stephen Clarkson shows how we have persistently mythologized about the true nature of our relationship with the Americans and have been too complacent about protecting our own interests. While we were busy deluding ourselves about our role as international peacekeeper and quiet diplomat, we allowed the process of continental integration to continue largely unchecked. Now we must recognize our dependency for what it is and work to change it.

Within Canada itself, we must seriously examine and assess the consequences of our dependency on American-dominated trade unions. In the face of the growing power of the multi-national corporations, many Canadian workers have already become aware of themselves as tiny parts of huge institutions, with little power to improve their conditions other than demanding higher wages and more fringe benefits. Discouraging more radical change is the fact that many belong to American-dominated international unions which discourage most attempts to decrease worker alienation through such policies as greater worker control and less routinized methods of production. Recently, however, American labour has been demanding that the American government encourage the multinationals to return jobs to the United States, thereby threatening the welfare of Canadian workers. Paul Phillips writes about this crisis in "Canadian Labour and the New Industrial State" and shows the importance of independent Canadian unions.

In attempting to understand and meet the challenge of our dependency, we must also consider that the challenge to our future does not originate solely from outside Canada, and all solutions do not simply involve stopping certain forces at the border. Within Canada itself, if we cannot formulate relevant alternatives which meet the dangers of both dependency and technique, then we can expect many Canadians to question the legitimacy of Canada itself. This is particularly true for the people of Quebec, where many now regard an independent Quebec as the only means by which French Canadians can assure their survival. In "Industrialization, Technology and Contemporary French-Canadian Nationalism," Edouard Cloutier traces the development of the nationalist movements in Quebec and shows why the Parti Québécois regards an independent Quebec as more significant than an independent Canada in meeting the cultural dangers of the technological society.

Wallace Gagne

Technology and Canadian Politics

To be Canadian is to recognize that ours is an existence without great purpose. Greatness is something we usually associate with the British and the Americans—Rule Britannia and Peace with Honour. In place of greatness we have opted for comfortable survival. In place of identity we have a fuzzy sense of "being different" without really knowing why. In place of nationalism we have a sense of internationalism which usually translates itself into continentalism. Given these characteristics, it is not surprising that Canadians have seldom displayed a desire for independence which has been translated into real political action. In part, these characteristics themselves arise from the impact of technology and technological change on our society.

This essay is an attempt to show how technology has contributed to the problem of Canada's existence, especially in the way it affects our politics. (Here I use the term technology in the general sense to refer both to the physical means of production and to the norms and values which organize and direct that productive system.) The first part of the essay will discuss the meaning of technology, relying particularly on the thought of Martin Heidegger. The second part will examine the impact of technology on Canadian politics, with particular emphasis on the problem of national independence.

9

TECHNÉ AND TECHNIQUE

In all the writings about technology, few authors have written as profoundly as Martin Heidegger. According to Heidegger, modern technology arose through a series of changes in philosophical and scientific thought which occurred primarily in the seventeenth century in western Europe. At the root of these changes lay the new view of nature as a resource to be exploited through rational methods. This contrasted sharply with the traditional conception of nature, and man's relationship to it, which came mainly from the ancient Greeks. In order to understand the meaning of modern technology, it is necessary to understand the nature of this philosophical change and how it led to modern technological society.

To the Greeks, nature meant the order in the universe. All things, from the inanimate to the divine, were part of this order and were distinguished from one another by their natures. Men were distinguished from animals by their reason and from the gods by the fact that they were creatures. For men to know what is good, they must contemplate the nature of the universal order and then act in terms of it; only in this way can they attune their actions to the universal harmony.

From this cosmological philosophy, the Greeks derived a system of values on which to base their conception of technology. This system of values they called techné and it is distinct from technique, which is the value system underlying modern technology. By comparing techné and technique, the meaning of modern technological society becomes clearer.

According to Heidegger, if we are to understand techné we must understand it in both a practical sense, and in terms of its essence.[1] Practically, techné is an instrumental activity of man involving means for achieving goals. Techné consists of the construction and use of tools and machines—the construction and use itself and also the goals which it serves. While the instrumental representation of techné is correct, it does not disclose the essence of techné and hence does not disclose its true meaning.

For the Greeks, the essence of techné was the unconcealing of truth; that is, it is a way of letting something "free to come forth." According to Aristotle, however, techné is a particular way of unconcealing. It unconceals those things which do not unconceal or produce themselves. Thus it refers both to manual activity and to artistic activity, but not to self-expression. For example, the person who builds a house unconceals the essence of "house" by joining together the material and the appearance of the house with the completely envisioned final product. In this way, instrumental activities were not merely processes of construction or personal aggrandizement, but were regarded by the Greeks as meaningful processes which were part of a greater cosmic order.

With the decline of Greek civilization, techné declined as well. In the Roman and Christian world, production came to be seen as an instrumental process for providing goods and services, rather than a means of revealing truth. The excesses of production, however, were checked by the belief in natural law and the desire to maintain harmony. Gradually, these too declined and man's conception of nature slowly changed from one of divinely ordained, natural hierarchy, to one of contingency of powers in which man was superior by virtue of his intellect and not by virtue of his spiritual being. It was from this new conception of nature that technique was derived.

Heidegger contends that to understand the nature of technique we must determine both its practical meaning and its essence. Practically, technique is similar to techné, in that it is an instrumental activity of man involving means for achieving goals. However, the essence is quite different. Whereas the essence of techné is unconcealing of truth, the essence of technique is *Gestell*, which provokes man to unconceal the actual in the way of employment as resource.

Gestell itself is nothing technical in the sense of a lever or an assembly line; rather it is that perception of nature as potential instrumentality which precedes the development of all particular technical organization:

Modern man takes the entirety of Being as raw material for production and subjects the entirety of the object world to the sweep and order of production (Herstellen). . . . the use of machinery and the production of machines is not technics itself but merely an adequate

instrument for the realization (Einrichtung) of the essence of technics
in its objective raw material.[2]

Unconcealing remains part of technique, but it is the unconcealing of energy through strip-mining and atom-smashing.

Heidegger illustrates the difference between ancient techné
and modern technique by contrasting a windmill with a hydro-
electric plant. Previously, the windmill could be used to derive
energy from nature by using the force of the wind to power
simple mechanical operations. However, this could only happen
when the wind blew, and so nature was still the master. Now,
man can use an instrument like the power plant to derive energy
and use it whenever he pleases:

> The unconcealing which pervades modern technic has the character
> of employing in the sense of provocation. This happens through the
> unlocking of the energy concealed in nature, the transforming of that
> which is unlocked, the storing of that which is transformed, the
> redividing up of that which is stored, and the switching over anew of
> that which is divided up.

Unlocking, transforming, storing, dividing up and switching
over are ways of unconcealing and are the processes which typify
modern technology.

In the modern era, nature is regarded as a storehouse of resources, of things which are employable for further employment:

> The coal demanded in the coal region is not employed so that it may
> be only generally and anywhere at hand. It stores, that is, it is in place
> (surstelle) for the employment of the sun's warmth stored in it. The
> sun's warmth is provoked for heat which is given the job of yielding
> steam whose pressure drives the works through which a factory
> remains in operation.[3]

Within this process, man's harmony with nature disappears as
he violates nature and forces her to yield energies and pleasures.

Growth of Technique through Science and Industry
The first significant manifestation of *Gestell* was the develop-
ment of modern natural science in the seventeenth century.
This was only possible after man represented nature as a con-

tingency of powers rather than as a chain of being. In this new representation, formal and final causes are discarded, and nature is regarded as a system of objects whose relationships can be calculated.[4] Nature is understood by positing hypotheses which are capable of empirical disconfirmation and which, if not falsified, can lead to the development of scientific theory. This positivist theory provides man with the theoretical knowledge necessary to control and to exploit nature through technology, particularly by employing methods which are not intuitively obvious, such as nuclear fission.

The next, and most familiar, manifestation of *Gestell*, was the Industrial Revolution, which began in the second half of the eighteenth century in Great Britain. Here, man mounted the most comprehensive and rational (instrumentally rational) attempt to exploit nature which had yet been seen. Instrumentally, the Industrial Revolution consisted of three main processes: the substitution of mechanical devices for human skills; the substitution of inanimate power (particularly steam) for human and animal strength; and a marked improvement in obtaining and working raw materials.[5] In social terms, the Industrial Revolution marked the decline of agrarianism and the beginning of modern urban society.

It was not accidental that industrialization should begin in Britain. In attempting to explain why, many authors have advanced arguments involving supply and demand factors: availability of coal and iron, proximity to market, need for military supplies, and so on. Others have argued in terms of theological beliefs which coincided with certain values and behaviour patterns considered conducive for capitalist expansion (Tawney and Weber). Obviously, these factors were important, and no explanation of the Industrial Revolution can ignore them. However, one factor appears paramount—the freedom of enterprise existing within Britain at this time. This freedom permitted industrial capitalism to come forth from the existing economic and social forces.

In writing about the nature of economic freedom at this time, Peter Mathias asserts that "the state had its back turned to the economy, as far as directly promoting industrial growth or new industrial skills on any scale were concerned."[6] In this atmosphere of salutary neglect, the newly emerging industrialists were able to manipulate the economic and social changes to their own advantage and, in the process, build up the basic structures of industrial capitalism. Thus, to the industrial capitalist, freedom meant access to capital and resources, unregulated markets, and the power to use the masses as a resource—industrial labourers. In most other countries, even those where the level of economic development was sufficient to facilitate industrialization, such as France and Germany, social organization and political control prevented the logic of industrial capitalism from developing.

Eventually the Industrial Revolution spread to the continent, then to North America and, more recently, to Asia and Africa. Usually the pattern of industrialization involved greater public initiative and imported capital than was the case in Britain.[7] In every case, however, nature was regarded as a resource, and it was from this premise that economic, social and political factors were used to promote the exploitation of nature through industrial production.

Gestell, *Technique and the Development of Canada*

Even before *Gestell* became manifest in science and industry, it stimulated the voyages of discovery which led to the colonization of the Americas. Initially, these voyages were designed to promote exploitation of the treasures of the East. This hope gradually faded and exploitation of the New World replaced it. Some, such as the Spanish and Portuguese, used conquest for plunder and quick profit: loot, slaves and tribute. Other European powers—France and Great Britain—chose to convert their conquests into enduring sources of wealth by establishing "plantations" and colonies.[8]

In New France, once the explorers discovered that the Huron were not the Inca, they began looking for alternate sources of wealth. What they found were furs, fish and farming. In order to develop these resources, it was necessary to survive the hostile elements and then to subdue the Indian and use him as a resource in the fur trade.[9] Once these two goals were achieved, the staples industries developed and the Empire of the St. Lawrence came into being. From its origins, therefore, Canada was regarded by others as a resource, and the people who settled here saw the production of resources as necessary for their survival and economic well-being.

This attitude grew stronger after the British conquest. The influx of British merchants, and later the United Empire Loyalists, injected greater economic rationality and a more aggressive commercialism into the development of Canada. After 1800 the collapse of the fur trade and the ensuing decline of the St. Lawrence Empire meant that new resources had to be found. Timber and an expanded agricultural base met this need. Commerce also expanded, and increasingly the course of development came under the influence of banks, land companies and canal companies.

At this time, the link between government and private commercial interests which was to control much of the future development of Canada was established. The politicians recognized that aggressive economic development was necessary for national development. In addition, the growth of liberal democracy meant that the mass demand for jobs and an increased standard of living would have to be met if politicians were to remain in office. Cooperation between government and private commerce to promote economic development thus became a traditional feature of Canadian politics.[10]

The commercial interests saw the link with government as a means of developing economic infrastructure at public expense, and also as a means of restricting competition through such devices as high tariffs. While the public purse financed roads, canals and railways, the merchants were free to invest their capital in less risky, and more profitable, endeavours such as land speculation. Between 1830 and 1867 canals were built by governments, and railroads by private corporations with the aid of government grants and guarantees.[11] Most of the capital for these projects was raised on the London money market by the legislatures concerned, and when some projects such as the canals failed to produce the expected profits, it was the public which paid for the losses.

The economic and political changes which arose through *Gestell* and technique affected much of the world after 1840. In British North America they upset the colonial economies, produced political instability and helped produce Confederation. After 1840 it became clear that those nations which were able to dominate the more advanced stages of technique would command tremendous political power. In contrast, those which were merely resource bases would be weak and dependent. While Britain and the northern United States were growing powerful through unlocking, transforming, storing, dividing up and switching over, the colonies of British North America were struggling to move beyond the unlocking stage.[12] As long as they remained tied to resource extraction, they knew they would remain subordinate within the empire.

Canada's dependence on resource extraction was the result of several factors. British mercantilism saw Canada as a source of raw materials and agricultural products, and as a captive market for British manufactured goods. Consequently, Britain discouraged colonial industrialization, either by specific laws or by retarding the migration of technology and technicians. Another factor discouraging colonial industrialization was the domination of merchant capital over industrial capital, which concentrated capital in the short-term, low-risk, staples enterprises.[13] Accordingly, in the 1850s most of the manufacturing industry was scattered in small units through the towns and villages of agricultural settlements. Only after the railways spread was there a tendency to increase unit size and concentrate in strategic centres.[14]

The repeal of the Corn Laws in 1846 removed the imperial preference which Canadian agricultural products entering the British market had enjoyed. This contributed to a depression in the colonies and emphasized the vulnerability of their narrowly based economies. In the face of this crisis, a two-part strategy gradually emerged to stimulate growth by expanding commerce. Part of this strategy involved the Reciprocity Treaty of 1854 which aimed at expanding trade by allowing for free trade in natural products with the United States, while permitting American manufactures to enter Canada. The second part of the strategy sought to expand trade by increasing commercial integration with the interior of the continent by building canals and railways. While the Reciprocity Treaty stimulated commerce, the latter strategy failed to capture the trade of the American Middle West, and instead created a debt amounting to almost 60 per cent of provincial and municipal debt in 1866.

Confederation, Nationalism and Foreign Investment

The men who gathered in Charlottetown in 1864 knew that unless they came to terms with the United States, there would be little chance of developing a strong and independent Canadian nation. To the south, the power of technique was being revealed as the northern states slowly crushed the Confederacy with factories and fire-power. All knew that Canada's sympathy with the rebels would end reciprocity, and might encourage expansionism into the northwest once the war was over. In addition, Britain now asserted that Canada must be largely responsible for her own security.[15] Despite Britain's indifference, the Fathers of Confederation still resolved to found "a great British Monarchy, in connection with the British Empire, and under the British Queen."[16] However, it would be a monarchy aimed at developing strength by imitating the American pattern of economic development.

None grasped this possibility more firmly than did Macdonald. He observed how waves of immigrants, swept to the expanding American frontier, had helped stimulate the industrial expansion of the northeast. In order to achieve this for Canada he sought to develop a strong central government which would build a transcontinental railroad, bring in immigrants and encourage industry through protective tariffs. Thus, political integration would be used to promote economic integration which was necessary for Canadian nationhood. In order to achieve political integration, Macdonald proposed a legislative union of the British North American colonies.

The political reality of Canada made legislative union impossible. Neither Quebec nor the Maritimes would agree to a scheme which would submerge their identity and autonomy. Nevertheless, the Fathers still believed that they had achieved a strong federal union by assigning seemingly insignificant powers to the provinces, and by vesting residual powers with the federal government, and giving it control of tariffs, the chief source of public revenue at the time. Later developments, both in the Judicial Committee of the Privy Council and in the nature of the Canadian economy, eventually eroded these measures and political power slipped back to the regions and provinces. Provincial control over natural resources such as minerals, hydroelectric power and petroleum products was strengthened and provided the basis for trade with the United States and for investment of American capital.[17]

Between 1867 and 1872 Confederation appeared to be working. Despite the end of reciprocity in 1866, exports to the United States increased by almost 30 per cent, industry was expanding, and the Intercolonial Railway was built. Then in 1873 a world depression began which lowered primary product prices and dried up investment capital. This led to a decline in Canadian exports and forced postponement of the transcontinental railway.[18]

Testimony before a Select Committee of the House of Commons in 1876 revealed the two opposing solutions to the problem of industrialization and economic development which were to endure as basic issues in Canadian politics. The most preferred solution was unrestricted reciprocity with the United States. Failing this, many wanted protection in the home market. Reciprocity was preferred because it would supposedly increase the flow of exports to the United States and permit rationalization of the Canadian economy within a North American economy. Such a result would obviously benefit merchant capital which controlled staples production. However, if they couldn't get reciprocity the merchants wanted to be protected from the dumping of cheap American goods on the Canadian market, and also to use a tariff wall to encourage broad economic expansion within Canada.

In the election campaign of 1878 the Conservatives came out with their "National Policy of Protection." Renewal of reciprocity was impossible and Macdonald advocated "incidental" protection in order to stimulate Canadian industry and to provide finances for additional roads, canals and railways.[19] In submitting the new tariffs to Parliament in 1879, Macdonald's Minister of Finance insisted that:

the time has arrived when we are to decide whether we will simply be hewers of wood and drawers of water.

. . . The time has certainly arrived when we must consider whether we will allow matters to remain as they are, with the result of being an unimportant and uninteresting portion of Her Majesty's Dominions, or will rise to the position, which I believe Providence has destined us to occupy. . .[20]

Here then was a clear will to technique: obvious dissatisfaction with a slow rate of economic development and a strong desire for progress through industrial production.

In retrospect, the National Policy was only partially successful as an instrument for industrialization and nationalism. Between 1880 and 1900 the National Policy led to completion of the transcontinental railway in 1886, helped promote the growth of secondary manufacturing and contributed to substantial economic growth. Interestingly enough, Canadian GNP in per capita terms grew more rapidly than that of the United States during the 1880s.[21] However, the Canadian economy did not approach the American in terms of absolute size, and the more rapid growth of the United States during the 1890s undermined the significance of the National Policy as a "catch-up" device.

One of the key failures of the National Policy was that it did not quickly produce the waves of immigrants needed for western settlement. Between 1880 and 1900 immigration to Canada was exceeded by emigration, and the Canadian population grew by less than the natural rate of increase. In turn, the failure of the immigration and homestead policies delayed the growth of western agriculture as the new staples base, and also delayed the growth of a large domestic market. Key factors in these failures were higher income levels in the United States which continued to attract immigrants, and land monopolization in the Canadian West by the Canadian Pacific Railway, the Hudson's Bay Company and the North-West Land Company which discouraged immigration to Canada. Only after the closing of the American frontier did the Canadian West become attractive to immigrants. At that point, the transcontinental railway contributed significantly to the process of national growth.

The economic and political effects of the tariff have been the subject of considerable academic debate. Historians tend to see the National Policy as an invaluable instrument of nation-building, and regard economic nationalism as necessary for political independence and the creation of a national economy.[22] In contrast, Watkins argues that "the tariff created Canadian industry, but not necessarily Canadian entrepreneurship, and hence not necessarily under Canadian ownership and control."[23] Further to this, Naylor argues that "attracting foreign capitalists and branch plants was explicit policy, a mercantile device for capitalist accumulation, and its short-run effects were fully anticipated."[24] Essentially, however, the tariff contributed to only part of the problem of foreign ownership and control of the Canadian economy. In order to evaluate the significance of the National Policy and understand how foreign ownership became a problem in Canada, it is necessary to examine certain key developments in the British and North American economies from 1867 onward.

Prior to Confederation, foreign investment did not threaten Canadian independence. In 1867 there was only $200 million worth of foreign capital in Canada, of which $185 million was British portfolio investment, and $15 million was American direct investment.[25] Most of the British investment had been used to finance canals and railroads, and since it was in the form of bonds and debentures, its owners could not exercise direct control within the Canadian economy. Even though American investors retained direct control over their capital, it was spread thinly throughout the economy, and hence did not dominate particular economic sectors. Early American investment went into such areas as the Canadian lumber trade, a cotton mill which was founded in Sherbrooke in 1844, and copper and silver mining around Lake Superior in 1846.[26]

Throughout the nineteenth and early twentieth centuries, Great Britain remained the dominant force in world finance. Between 1870 and 1914, it is estimated that Britain's total capital exports amounted to some £3,500 million.[27] Almost all of it went into stable portfolio investments, both within the Empire and wherever investment opportunities arose. By 1913, Britain had exported almost $3 billion of portfolio investment to Canada. While this indebtedness presented a balance-of-payments problem for Canada, it did not create the same type of problems which were to come with increased American investments. The beginning of the First World War began the decline of British overseas investments. For Canada, this meant greater reliance on American capital, at first in the form of more portfolio investment, and later in terms of considerable direct investment.

In general, American influence in Canada increased as industrial capitalism expanded in the United States. Once the United States recovered from the Civil War, the American economy began a phenomenal process of industrial growth and concentration.[28] As an example of this process, Mandel points out that by 1900 America was the leading exporter of steel on the world market, and by 1913 she produced 40 per cent of the world's steel, more than that of France, Great Britain and Germany together.[29] Accompanying such growth was a need for markets and resources, and in both areas Canada proved most useful.

Between 1867 and 1900 American direct investment in Canada increased steadily. During those years, approximately $160 million of American capital was invested in the Canadian economy. By 1900, there were probably over a hundred companies in Canada which were controlled by or definitely affiliated with American firms, and American direct investment totalled about $175 million. From then on, American investment grew rapidly. By 1934 the list of companies had grown to more than 1,350 and American direct investment totalled over $2 billion. In terms of initial establishment in Canada, 5 per cent of these companies began operations before 1900, 11 per cent were established from 1900 to 1909, 22 per cent from 1910 to 1919, 36 per cent from 1920 to 1929 and 26 per cent from 1930 to 1934.[30]

Although the desire to profit was the main factor behind American investment in Canada, more specific factors in particular economic sectors were also significant. In the manufacturing sector, the tariff was obviously important. Many

American firms that wished to extend their sales to the Canadian market did so by establishing branch plants which not only helped to avoid the tariff, but also comforted consumers who wanted Canadian-made goods. In addition, American firms wishing to take advantage of the preferential tariff system of the British Empire found it economical to add "Canadian content" to their products and then export them accordingly. Thus, for example, in the 1920s, the Canadian branches of both Ford and General Motors exported large portions of their automobile production to Empire countries, in addition to supplying the Canadian market.

Considerable American investment in Canadian resources arose from the scarcity of particular resources in the United States, or their favourable location in relation to American industry. Canadians seemed unwilling or unable to develop these resources, and so Americans were welcomed both by governments which wanted development, and by Canadian entrepreneurs anxious to sell leases and other assets. An example was the International Nickel Company which was founded to develop nickel and copper deposits around Sudbury, and which sold virtually all of its nickel production in the United States or the international market, since there was little demand for nickel in Canada.

In the case of newsprint, American investment increased as timber resources declined in the United States. From 1910 onward, American money flowed into both privately owned timber land and leases of crown land. Simultaneously, provincial and federal legislation prohibiting the export of pulpwood from crown lands stimulated the development of American-owned pulp and paper mills in Canada to produce newsprint which could leave Canada freely and enter the United States duty-free. It is interesting to note that in 1933, the great house organ of American liberalism, the *New York Times,* through the Spruce Falls Power and Paper Company, held cutting rights on 4,700 square miles of Canadian timber, an area as large as Connecticut.[31]

Accompanying the growing American interest in Canadian mines and forests was a similar interest in Canadian energy. Part of this interest arose from the need to provide infrastructure for investments in other areas. Thus, in 1924 the International Paper and Power Company began developing extensive hydroelectric facilities on the Gatineau and Ottawa rivers through its Canadian Hydro-Electric Corporation, in order to serve its Canadian paper mills. Other firms, such as the Niagara-Hudson Power Corporation, developed power plants in Canada to harness energy for export to the United States. Ironically, most early American investment in Canadian oil and gas was geared to serve the Canadian market. In 1930 American petroleum companies in Canada had most of their money invested in the refining and distribution of petroleum products made from crude oil, 95 per cent of which was imported, 75 per cent of it coming from the United States.

Since the 1930s the volume of foreign investment in Canada has grown enormously.[32] Immediately after the Second World War, large amounts of U.S. direct investment flowed into resource industries, and then in the mid-1950s vast amounts poured into manufacturing. More recently, investors from such nations as France, Germany, Japan and Sweden have also begun to buy Canadian resources and properties.

Today, most of the economic and political effects of this massive influx of foreign capital are readily apparent. American ownership and control of much of Canada's resource production has encouraged its integration with the American industrial system, thereby tying Canada to the business cycles of the United States. Subordination of large segments of Canadian secondary industry within the structure of multinational corporations allows them to expand or truncate production to suit their own purposes. Regional disparities have been accentuated as foreign capital has promoted the rapid development of areas like southern Ontario, while ignoring areas such as the Maritimes. National unity has grown tenuous as regions compete among themselves for markets and investment. Finally, it is clear that a significant portion of Canada's resource and manufacturing potential is not being used to promote Canada's national interests, but instead to serve American corporate interests.

Rather than oppose this process, Canada's leaders have given it active encouragement. Most still firmly believe in the power of technique, and trust that enormous human good will arise through the continual conquest of nature and the development of resources. In the past, men such as King, Howe and Duplessis became enmeshed in the development syndrome and did everything possible to encourage foreign investment. American investors, in particular, responded to favourable legislation, government concessions and discriminatory labour practices. Few Canadians saw any threat to their independence from this influx of outside money because they regarded the economic and political systems as largely separate, and believed that so long as Canadians maintained control of their own political institutions, Canada would remain independent. American money and technology would be used to develop Canada, and Americans would receive a "fair rate of return."

The most critical development which has served to undermine this naive conception of economics and politics has been the growth of the multinational corporation. In the case of Canada, these institutions became significant after 1918. Previously, most American direct investment came from national corporations which operated primarily in the United States and Canada. They tended to seek resources on a limited basis, or sought to operate in a narrow segment of the Canadian market. Since most were relatively small, they could not place much pressure on governmental institutions and were generally beneficial, since they provided needed capital and created jobs for Canadians. In many cases, American investors actually accompanied their capital to Canada.

After 1918, many firms that had operated on a binational basis gradually became multinational.[33] As such, they operated on a much larger scale and spread their activities across many economic sectors. In addition, they tended to integrate their decision-making much more tightly with the parent firm. As Canadians sought greater technological growth and development through these corporations, they found that the price was the loss of ownership and control of their own economy. Today, Canadians find themselves in a position where a majority of their manufacturing and resource production industries are now in American hands. As the following pages will show, the style of life and the type of politics which have evolved through technique make reversal of this process extremely complicated and perhaps impossible.

CANADIAN POLITICS AND CANADIAN INDEPENDENCE

Many people concerned with the question of Canadian independence regard it as a problem capable of political solution. Ideally they would like to see a National Policy of independence to ensure that Canada's economy and resources serve Canadian interests, while using Canada's educational and communications systems to preserve and promote a national Canadian identity. Some see nationalization of multinational corporations and social ownership of the means of production as necessary pre-conditions for achieving these objectives, while others would be content with various forms of screening agencies and quotas. Whatever their methods, however, I believe most forms of traditional nationalism[34] offer a false hope, for not only are most nationalist policies impossible to implement, but I do not believe they would achieve their desired goals even if implemented.

In an immediate sense, traditional nationalism is unworkable in Canada because Canadians do not wish to exist as a nation. Our politics are not based on a common nationality derived from common myths, values or ethnic background. Rather, Canada exists as a compendium of ethnic, communal and regional groups, loosely joined in a federal system. No great national identity holds us together and gives us direction, but instead a mutual respect of difference expressed through such concepts as bilingualism or multiculturalism helps engender various forms of voluntary cooperation. Only in times of dire emergency have we been willing to concentrate political power in the hands of a strong central government. It is little wonder, therefore, that many regard what passes for Canadian nationalism as essentially anti-Americanism, since it is not primarily based on a single conception of nation, but more often reflects a reaction against homogenization by American culture and economic power.

The fact that Canada is more federal than national means that policies for the whole of Canada are extremely difficult to implement. Any attempt by Ottawa to formulate the type of policies and exert the type of control necessary to achieve economic independence for Canada would face strong resistance from the provinces which are striving to retain whatever control they still have over their economies. Alberta, for example, would fight any attempt by Ottawa to take over the oil industry, while Newfoundland would similarly resist federal control over the iron ore of Labrador. Not only would such attempts by Ottawa be interpreted as exceeding the basic federal agreement in Canada, but they would also be seen as an attempt by the province of Ontario to gain greater power and economic benefits for itself through the federal government.

In a more profound sense, however, nationalism is unworkable because for most Canadians it holds no meaning. Essentially, this is what George Grant argues in *Lament for a Nation,* in which he shows how men who equate their fate with the dynamism of technology find nothing attractive in something as conservative as nationalism because they see little in the past that is worthy of preservation. In this regard, Canadians are more like the Americans than they care to admit. There are, however, certain real differences between Canadians and Americans which still exist, differences which can be used as the basis for maintaining certain types of detachment from America, and for building a way of life for Canadians that holds more meaning than the mindless pleasure-seeking of the technological society. It is important therefore to consider what these differences are and to see how they can be used to build a new and meaningful politics.

Canadian Political Ideology and Identity

The men who settled America came to win freedom and enjoy prosperity. For them, the American Revolution signified not only the defeat of British imperialism, but also the end of any type of Tory restraint on individual freedom or material progress.[35] Henceforth, any conception of an organic society based on hierarchical principles was politically unacceptable, and any type of communal restraint on individual freedom was regarded as un-American. Today, liberalism remains the one true myth in the United States. Whether it is the classical liberalism of a Barry Goldwater or the New Left liberalism of a George McGovern, political debate occurs largely within the framework of how best to maximize freedom and promote prosperity. Even a policy as abhorrent as that in Southeast Asia has been debated almost entirely within the liberal ethos, with some Americans defending American actions there as necessary to protect freedom in the world, and others condemning the policy for undermining the domestic freedom of Americans because of the way in which it was created and executed.

Before any other nation, the Americans successfully joined together liberalism and technique as the basis of a national political culture. For Americans, the desire for egalitarianism and material progress made liberalism and technique highly compatible. The liberal beliefs that man's essence is his freedom and that life is an open-ended progression in which men will be endlessly free to make the world as they want it, made technique not only acceptable, but morally necessary. By conquering nature through science and technology, man attains greater power and resources which permit both greater choice about the future and greater equality of opportunity for the under-privileged. Thus liberalism encourages technique to unfold, and technique, in turn, permits greater freedom.

The fact that most Americans considered the right to liberty to be higher than any single conception of the good also enhanced the pervasiveness of liberalism and the sheer dynamism of American society.[36] The priority of right to good meant that Americans should not try to move towards an ideal society, but rather should concentrate on protecting and expanding individual freedom, since this was the best possible way of uplifting the individual and protecting him from tyranny and intolerance. In addition, the priority of right meant that no conception of the good could be used to restrain the progress of technique. Only if the excesses of technique seriously threatened individual liberty was there a moral justification for impeding progress; even this restraint was difficult to exercise, since the newly emerging society was little given to contemplation.

Besides excluding other ideologies, the priority of right also

contributed to the homogenization of ethnic and religious identities into the dominant liberal-technical ethos. The latecomers
to America soon learned that ethnic cultures were foreign and
irrational in America, since they supposedly produced the type
of nationalist intolerance and violence which had initially
forced the immigrant to leave his homeland. Ideally, such cultures should best be forgotten, or failing this, sublimated
throughout one's workday and brought out after-hours as a
means of relaxation or as curiosities for the neighbours. Quite
naturally, most people chose to adopt the competitive, commercial values of American mass society and attain the same
influence as their rivals, rather than fight to preserve an identity
which was regarded as un-American and which often proved
incompatible with material success. Thus America began and
evolved as a nation of individual calculators rather than one in
which group values gave people meaning and identity. While
Americans continue to make much of the cultural, racial and
regional differences within America, these differences are merely
superficial and what really counts politically is the dominance
of technique and liberalism.

In time, Americans came to believe that they were the one
people who had attained human greatness without having resorted to nationalism or other extreme forms of self-interest.
They also came to regard theirs as the one true plural society,
the society in which men of all colours and creeds were free to
live as they chose. The past century, however, has demonstrated
the falsity of these beliefs and revealed the true nature of
American liberal-nationalism, which uses the "protection of
freedom" to justify American self-interest and the "promotion
of progress" as an apology for economic imperialism. It is little
wonder, therefore, why so many have come to despise the Americans and their account of freedom, and why many of the other
inhabitants of North America now fear and question their
dominance of the continent.

According to George Grant, much of what North America is
today arose from the nature of its primal origins, which involved "the meeting of the alien and yet conquerable land with
English-speaking Protestants."[37] This meeting opened the way

for the growth of both liberalism and technique and instilled a sense of moral purpose in those who began the rational conquest of man and nature in the name of freedom.

For Canadians, the primal was not just the meeting of the land with European calculators, but also the meeting of French-speaking Roman Catholics with English-speaking Protestants. The fact of this dual primal means that in many ways we are like the Americans, but in others we are quite different. We, too, embody many of the liberal and technical values which dominate American life, but we differ in the fact that these values have not produced a national political culture in Canada which dominates our lives as such a culture dominates American life. Much of this difference lies in the fact that, from 1759 onwards, two quite distinct peoples, the English and the French, were forced to coexist in a spirit of mutual toleration. No single set of values could be used to form a homogeneous national culture, but rather the constant tension between the two peoples helped maintain a bicultural society, which more recently has been giving way to a more multicultural form of society.

The most significant factor maintaining the bicultural nature of Canada during our formative years was the determination of French Canadians to survive as a distinct ethnic and cultural community within North America. Not only did this counter the amalgamating efforts of English Canadians, many of whom sought to achieve Lord Durham's recommendation of a "complete amalgamation of peoples, races, languages and laws," but also countered the homogenizing forces of technique and American liberalism. The contest between English and French was not always on an equal basis, of course, since the English Canadian enjoyed superiority of numbers and much greater economic and industrial power. In cultural terms, however, the French Canadian enjoyed an advantage since his language, history and traditions were quite distinct within North America, and provided him with an identity and purpose to life which the English Canadian could not always understand and appreciate or discover for himself.

In contrast to the French Canadian, the English Canadian has not appeared particularly distinctive in relation to the American, partly because the cultures of both developed from the common British traditions of empiricism, utilitarianism and industrialism. These values, together with a similar belief in liberalism and technique, cause many French Canadians to regard English Canadians as so many barbarians who live only for money and status. Despite this similarity, however, there are significant differences between the English Canadian and the American which stem from differences in historical, social and cultural beliefs.

The identity of the English Canadian originates in the fact that, from the Loyalists onwards, British people coming to Canada have always regarded British culture and institutions as better than the American. British immigrants believed they were coming to a society here that was essentially British, and which did not suffer from the excesses of egalitarianism and republicanism. Even though their motive in coming to Canada may have been material, this did not mean they had to become just like the Americans in order to attain success. To them, Canada was orderly and sensible, while America was chaotic and uncultured. Thus, although they shared many basic values with the American, they believed that they were different from him and that it was important to maintain those differences. Consequently, at times when the question of Canada's relationship with the United States was actually raised as a political issue, such as the reciprocity election of 1911, Tory politicians found they had a reservoir of British and Canadian loyalty to draw upon among English Canadians.

Today when we use the term English Canadian, we usually refer not only to those of Anglo-Saxon or British origin, but generally to all whose principal language is English. Essentially, this latter usage is misleading since it often implies a degree of cultural or social homogeneity among "English Canadians" which usually does not exist. The origins and values of Irish "English Canadians" or Polish "English Canadians" are obviously quite different from those of the original "English Canadian," and members of these other groups find meaning and identity in many ways in which the Anglo-Saxon does not, particularly through their religions and their folklore. In recent years, many of these people, together with many French Canadians, have been challenging the social and political hegemony of the Anglo-Saxon in Canadian life, with the result that there has been greater official recognition paid to biculturalism, and even multiculturalism. Generally, however, the Anglo-Saxon remains dominant in many significant spheres and we are not likely to see the end of the vertical mosaic within our lifetimes. It is significant, however, that even though the Anglo-Saxon has been dominant in many areas, he has never been able to mould a national culture in his own image, with the result that Canada still consists of not just one but many natures.

In thinking about our future and about the question of Canadian independence, therefore, we must begin by recognizing the collectivity of identities within Canada. Only by first accepting this fact can we work towards an independence policy which will be accepted by most Canadians. Only in this way can we avoid aiming at false targets such as trying to establish a distinctive national identity or an unhyphenated Canadianism which will make all of us distinct from the Americans, but all in the same way. Not only would such a goal threaten most non-Anglo-Saxons, it would be absurd to believe that we could legislate a national culture which is consistent with the human considerations we all wish to preserve. Rather we must search for those economic and political policies which are consistent with our cultural diversity and attempt to adopt those which best serve our goals of self-determination.

The Communal Nature of Canadian Politics

Another factor which distinguishes Canadian from American society, and which is closely tied to our multiculturalism, is the widespread existence of communities and communal values throughout Canada. In Canada today, we still find many groups of people who look primarily to their immediate fellows for meaning and identity, who regard cultural and traditional values more highly than material progress, and attempt to relate to each other in cooperative rather than competitive ways.

Evidence of the greater importance of communal values in Canadian society range from such broad considerations as our earlier acceptance of medicare, which benefits the community generally, to more specific concerns such as OFY and LIP grants, which are designed to foster communal concerns at the local level. In addition, Canadians are more concerned about such everyday things as keeping the streets clean and maintaining one's home, not only for practical reasons, but also to protect the well-being of the community. In contrast, Americans still allow the marketplace to determine the quality of health care for most people, still regard cultural and ethnic minorities as political interest groups to be bought off rather than accepted as part of a wider community, and now see law and order as the only means left to preserve urban life.

Even though most communities in Canada sprang from economic necessity, many different forms of community have persisted as significant social and political forces long after the economic reasons for their creation have disappeared. In the United States, most forms of community were replaced by the structures and values of American mass society once the economic necessity of community disappeared. In part, this difference reflects the greater dynamism and pragmatism of American life, but it also reflects differences in the historical development as well as the social and political values of each country.

Throughout this century Canadian communal values have been under increasing pressure from liberalism and technique, with the result that many of the traditional forms of community, such as small-town life, have withered or disappeared. Despite this fact, many of the communal values are still alive, and as Canadians increasingly realize the dangers of living in a society in which human meaning is dissolving and excess cannot be restrained, it is hoped that they will turn to new forms of community values to regain meaning and to live life in a more reasonable and sensible fashion. Here, the important point is that Canadians have a communal base on which to build, and even though it varies among the regions of Canada, it can be used to develop a way of life that is both meaningful and independent of American mass society and American economic control.

In looking, first, at the communal base of the Maritimes, one of the most striking features of community in this region is the way it has survived for the past two centuries. This is explained in part by the pride of the Maritimers in their unhurried, distinctive way of life, and by the lack of aggressive economic development and large influxes of new people to threaten the traditional ways. Generally, the pattern of migration has been outward, particularly as young Maritimers realized the lack of economic opportunities at home. These realities made for a stable form of communal society, in which those who stayed in the Maritimes looked to each other for meaning and identity, and in which local customs and traditions, along with local feuds and grievances, remained intact. Thus, communal cultures such as the Irish Canadian of Newfoundland, the Scottish Canadian of Nova Scotia, and the French Canadian of New Brunswick have survived and flourished. For many, however, it is a losing battle and they have given up the fight and moved to Montreal or Toronto, there to live in high-rise apartments, sell encyclopedias and join societies of expatriate Maritimers.

Recently there has been a concerted effort by Ottawa and by Maritime governments to stimulate the economic development of the region. These attempts have created a dilemma for many Maritimers because they realize that, on the one hand, if the culture and communities of the region are to survive, the region must retain its young people by providing them with good jobs and a decent standard of living. On the other hand, they realize that the only practical way of achieving these goals at present is to build Volvo plants and super-tanker ports. The costs of such developments in social terms could be the destruction of local communities and the creation of alienated urban concentrations. In addition, the contemporary form of economic development could well serve to integrate the Maritimes with central Canada and the United States as a mere appendage of their industrial systems, as well as intensify the problems created by the massive influx of foreign capital. Collectively, these policies could take control of the economy out of local hands and destroy the independent spirit of the region, unless much greater attention is paid to how and when to encourage development.

Generally, the forces of development have dominated because

most Canadians believe that growth is the only realistic way of improving their material existence and preventing the decay of their region. Most attacks on development have been ineffective because they have come long after the development process has been put in motion and have attacked only the peripheries of development in non-essential ways, such as limiting the height of high-rises or shifting the location of airports.

Politically it is extremely difficult to prevent major development projects such as the James Bay power project because the vested interests are much more powerful than their opponents and have much greater influence with governments, regulatory agencies, the courts and public opinion. In this process industry, labour and even government itself cooperate to encourage development: industry wants profits, labour wants jobs, and government wants to keep voters happy by providing prosperity, with the result that the anti-development forces find a united elite against them, particularly in times of economic crisis. As a consequence, development itself is not a serious issue within Canadian politics, although the way it is to be achieved often is, since all do not share the benefits or bear the costs on an equal basis. Under these conditions it would be absurd to attempt to formulate an independence policy based on anti-development. Rather, we must attempt to relate future development to existing communities in such a way that the communities are given the economic means to survive and so that as much control as possible resides in the hands of the community.

None are as acutely aware of the problems of technological development and the threats which they pose to cultural and communal survival as the people of Quebec. Here, these issues have been part of life since before the Conquest and it is hardly necessary to describe again the traditional desire of French Canadians to survive as a distinct group, and the price they have paid for that survival in terms of lost economic opportunities and loss of their compatriots to the mills and factories of the United States. Now the question is whether French Canada can survive within North America, or whether it will become like the rest of the continent, where most people have surrendered distinctiveness for progress and modernity. Much of the current debate over the future of French Canada comes down to the question of whether Quebec should remain part of the Canadian federal system and attempt to maintain its distinctiveness there, or follow a path of greater or even complete independence and attempt to shape its destiny unfettered by the ties and shackles of the rest of Canada.

Whichever course Quebeckers choose, it is clear that the threat to their culture will be tremendous. Should they choose to remain within Canada, then they must face continued exploitation by the English-speaking economic elite, greater cultural assimilation, and the hostility of many Canadians opposed even to such piecemeal programs as bilingualism and biculturalism. In attempting to provide for the future of Quebeckers and keep the province within Canada, Quebec governments, together with the federal government, have resorted to the massive development of resources such as iron ore, asbestos, hydro and transportation in the hope that these will raise living standards and keep the masses content. In addition, significant attempts have been made to modernize and liberalize the education system, provide greater technical training, and rationalize the public bureaucracy.

While it can be argued that these changes are necessary in an economic and technical way, it must also be realized that little consideration has been given to their long-term effects on French Canadians as a people. The general approach has been to develop and modernize as much as possible, while paying only lip-service to the question of cultural survival by building arts centres, subsidizing sculptors and insisting on French names for American-owned hotels. The consequence of such a one-sided emphasis on development will be the end of French Canada's distinctiveness, for even if the French language is preserved, it can make little cultural or social difference if everyone lives in the same type of apartment, works for the same type of corporation and defines himself in terms of the same technical values as most others in North America.

At present, the main alternative to the liberal-technocratic approach is the semi-socialist, semi-separatist program of the

Parti Québécois, who hope to gain control of the Quebec economy through peaceful political means. They then hope to use this power to direct and control technology along those paths most favourable to French survival. If experience elsewhere can be any guide, it would appear that this may be a futile hope. In immediate terms, the question of whether technology can be controlled as people wish is an extremely difficult and complex one to answer. It cannot be answered solely in terms of controlling the means of production or moulding the pattern of development to one's tastes. The usual consequence of encouraging growth and development is to forgo economic independence and integrate the domestic economy with the wider economic and technological systems outside of one's state which are necessary to sustain the technological process. Even the United States with its vast storehouse of wealth has had to face energy shortages and monetary crises which have served to undermine its independence. Under the present circumstances, there is little reason to believe that an "independent" Quebec could really be independent if it chooses to follow the technological development course towards mass prosperity. Furthermore, there is little reason at present to believe that the French-Canadian masses would support a movement which would have them forgo prosperity for cultural survival. As yet the question of how French Canadians should seek to maintain their distinctiveness remains unanswered, and it will require considerably more thought before it is.

Across the border in Ontario the process of cultural erosion and technological homogenization has gone much farther than in Quebec, with the result that many of the things which once made Ontario distinctive have now been lost. This one-time centre of British Empire loyalties became the first region of Canada to welcome American investment on a grand scale once the British connection lost its fiscal attractiveness. In a sense, the economic integration of southern Ontario and American industry was almost inevitable, since this part of Canada fits so comfortably into the American industrial heartland running from Chicago, through Cleveland and Detroit, across upper New York State and on down to New York City and Boston.

What better way to develop and to progress than by locking the steel mills of Hamilton, the factories of Oakville and the offices of Toronto into this great productive arch? It is this side of Ontario's existence which makes many Canadians in other regions fear and despise it and resent the influence which it exercises within the Canadian federal system.

The major question about Ontario is whether the process of economic and cultural assimilation with the United States can be reversed or whether Ontario will simply become more and more like its American counterparts. Many of the classic problems accompanying rapid urban growth are already here, with the result that many of those entombed in the apartment towers of Scarborough, North York and Mississauga see little to life other than making enough money at Imperial Oil or IBM to escape into privatization. Increasingly, more and more young people are being drawn into this lifeless form of existence which sees the future as little more than better job opportunities, cheaper land for more shoddy townhouses and better television sets to watch expansion hockey. It is little wonder, therefore, that Canadian independence and nationalism have little meaning for most of these people other than pasting maple leaf decals on their Samsonite luggage so that Europeans won't mistake them for Americans.

As yet, Ontario has not completely sold out its identity for growth and development. Among the factories, expressways and jug milk stores there still remains a sense of civility which distinguishes it from the American northeast. Urban decay and disorder remains in check largely by communal sensibilities, and occasionally the provincial Conservatives recall their Tory past sufficiently to curb the excesses of land developers or halt the construction of expressways. Then, too, it is important to consider that Ontario is not just an urban monolith. The communities of the north are quite distinct from the south, while smaller cities such as Dundas, Kingston and Stratford offer alternatives to the urban mass. Even that most hated of cities, Toronto, has experienced a cultural rejuvenation as more and more immigrants have invaded her WASP soul and established their own communities.

Another hopeful factor about Ontario is that many in the large urban centres have now realized the need to preserve the life of their city in the face of such urban disasters as Detroit and Buffalo. Whether this realization will be converted into a more personalized form of society and politics remains to be seen; however, the fact that the chances of chaos are now real may well stimulate significant change. Then, too, it is apparent that the other regions of Canada are now unwilling to accept Ontario's domination of Canadian federalism as passively as they once did. Provinces like Alberta and Quebec realize they have resources which are badly needed by the industrial heartland, and are now demanding higher prices and greater political influence as the price. Within this new context there is hope for negotiating a new deal for Canada, one in which the industrial heartland concept will be abandoned, and each region will be more self-sufficient.

In western Canada, communal values and structures are still deeply held, particularly in rural areas, but also in urban areas where many have inherited communal values from parents who lived in rural communities. Both on the prairies and in British Columbia, many different forms of religious, ethnic and economic communities still thrive: the Jews of North Winnipeg, the farmers of Saskatchewan, the Ukrainians of northeastern Alberta and the English of Victoria. In addition, westerners are tied together by a common sense of grievance and exploitation by central Canada, particularly Ontario. They believe that central Canada, historically, has monopolized economic and political power by establishing itself as the industrial heartland through such devices as the National Policy, and has assigned the West the role of resource producer and captive market. This sense of grievance has combined with the communal roots of the West to create a western identity which is producing a new sense of militancy within Canadian politics, and even some talk of western separatism.

Today, western Canada is assuming much greater significance in a resource-hungry world. Accompanying this change is a strong desire by many westerners to insure that most of the benefits from such things as British Columbia lumber, Alberta oil and prairie grain go to the people of western Canada. Increasingly these desires are being articulated to the rest of Canada, and to the rest of the world by the premiers of the western provinces who recognize the political advantages of such policies, as well as the real economic benefits which will accrue to the West if the western provinces can bargain collectively.

In coming to the bargaining table with the rest of Canada, therefore, westerners have both a sense of their own identity and a sense of the growing economic importance of the West. They are particularly concerned that if the federal government adopts national policies in the resource field, which are supposedly in the interests of all Canadians, westerners will be the ones who have to bear most of the costs. Too many times have the interests of the West been sacrificed for those of Ontario, all in the name of "Canadian nationalism." Thus, for example, when it comes to sharing western oil with Ontario, westerners want reciprocal action in terms of lower transportation costs and a real opportunity to develop secondary industry in order to diversify the western economy and prepare for the day when their non-renewable resources are exhausted.

While western resistance to economic exploitation is to be admired, there is a real danger that the western sense of grievance will produce little more than a desire for revenge against central Canada. Unfortunately, this sentiment has already blinded many westerners to the fact that American corporations also have enormous influence in the western economies, and those corporations have even less concern for the long-term interests of the region than do federal politicians or Canadian corporations. Rather than simply blaming Toronto and Ottawa for everything which goes wrong in western Canada, westerners must perceive their difficulties through a broader perspective by also recognizing the influence of the United States in their affairs. Unless they do so, they are unlikely to accomplish much of positive benefit for their society and will only become more embittered and disillusioned. At the same time, however, central and eastern Canadians must also begin to recognize the legitimacy of western grievances and adopt a more conciliatory attitude towards solving western problems.

TECHNOLOGY, INDEPENDENCE AND
THE FUTURE OF CANADA

Technique is now the most dominant and pervasive force direct-
ing the course of modern man. In following the path of technological development we have lost much of our independence as
Canadians. By continuing to follow that path we risk losing our
existence as men. This is the threat which faces us as we contemplate the future of Canada, and the reason why we must seek an
alternative to our present course.

The greatest danger of technique is that man will become
merely another resource in the technological process and lose
any opportunity of discovering his potential as man. As Heidegger argues, this threat does not come from technique itself,
which permits man to control the physical world, but from the
excesses of *Gestell* which provokes man to regard everything
as a resource to be exploited, including man himself. If men
regard one another as merely resources, then they cannot discover themselves as men, for it is they who will be dominated
by *Gestell* and lose sight of that higher unconcealing which is
the essence of man. Not only does regarding man as a resource
prevent him from discovering his essence, it also leads to the
unlimited exploitation of man by man. No excess against
human dignity is prohibited as long as it contributes to the
orderly working of the technological society. Thus, man is no
longer the master of technique but becomes an appendage of
the technological system.

While some concerned Canadians are now looking to political
means to overcome the domination of technique, it is clear that
as long as the present marriage of technique and political power
endures, our political system will offer no alternative to our
present course. Rather than challenging the excesses of technique, our political leaders and parties now increase its domination by promoting all forms of mindless progress and by
oppressing those who question the excesses. Both the Liberal
and Progressive Conservative parties are now dominated by
right-wing technocrats who see freedom and progress as the
most sacred of all values, and who are essentially interchange-
able as apologists for technique. The left-wing technocrats who

dominate the New Democratic Party are little different, for while they may question some of the excesses of capitalism, they too equate our destinies with freedom and progress, and would use greater state control to promote these objectives.

Politics in our society has now become an instrumental process in which polls, propaganda and image are used to gain power and to protect the system. Political philosophy has been largely rejected as the basis of political action, and has been replaced by ideology and political culture, which are much more compatible with calculation and manipulation. Rather than attempting to relate political action to a conception of a greater whole, decision-makers proceed incrementally, reflecting majority opinions and attitudes, and refusing to risk alternatives which might upset voters or corporate donors. It is little wonder, therefore, why many sensitive people now refuse to vote and have retreated from the political system. What this means, however, is that the political game will be left to the most ambitious and reactionary elements in our society, and if change is to occur, it will have to be sought in alternate ways.

Alternatives

Any attempt to change our present course must begin with a clear recognition of what has been lost in permitting technique to dominate our lives. At the most fundamental level, we have lost our awareness of the broad spectrum of feelings, beliefs and sensations which is the essence of life. Instead we have chosen to become western rational men by narrowing our consciousness to the instrumental aspects of reality. Rather than regarding life as an exciting possibility, we attempt to deny the disturbing and uncertain part of reality while seeking complete control and predictability. Lost in the process is any conception of the novelty of life or any attempt to discover its deeper meaning. Lost, too, is that openness which characterized earlier peoples and which today is found occasionally among more primitive peoples. Instead we are raised as rational men, trained to deny our fuller consciousness, and filled with the fears and paranoia that provoke us to sublimate ourselves into achievement and order.

It is from this distorted consciousness that we as Canadians have lost much of our independence and retreated into the technological society. It is from this distorted consciousness that we have created the economic, social and political structures which work against our human nature and which chain us to a meaningless existence. Before we can move beyond this state we must first become aware that we are in it. Only then can we begin changing the structures which bind us and start discovering the whole of our consciousness and living our lives as complete and open beings.

As Canadians, it is clear that we must change many existing relationships and open many new paths before we can reach a higher state of existence. An obvious starting point is our relationship with the United States.[38] Clearly we cannot permit the present course of American domination to continue if we hope to decide for ourselves how the resources and industries of Canada will be used to benefit Canadians and other peoples of the world. Without much greater control over our economy we will remain an appendage of the American industrial system, subject to all the worst features of that system, and unable to integrate our productive activities with other parts of our lives in ways of our own choosing.

In the past we have been extremely reluctant to challenge the economic domination of the Americans. Now, however, we live in a different world, in which America is no longer supreme, but, rather, must cooperate with other nations to enjoy continued prosperity. If anything, the Vietnamese war has demonstrated to the Americans and to all the world that technology is not sufficient to bend the weak to their will, and that, if they should consider using force to obtain scarce resources, the weak but determined peoples can raise the cost of those resources to impossible levels.[39] The assumption that the Americans can come into Canada and take whatever they need, should we prove reluctant to continue our present relationship with them, is a simple-minded belief which should no longer dominate our relationship with the United States.

It is now time Canadians realized that we are in a bargaining situation with the United States and our bargaining position has been improving dramatically as the quantity of American resources has declined. If we are sensible and courageous (I realize that these two qualities do not always mesh) we can assure a much better position for ourselves within North America. The most significant part of our present relationship with the United States which must be challenged is the unacceptably high degree of American ownership and control of the Canadian economy. Providing we pay the Americans reasonable compensation for their assets and permit them to bargain with other nations for resources which we choose to sell, then the transition from American to Canadian control could be relatively painless. We won't know for sure, of course, until we try, but if we don't begin very soon then the time for trying could well run out as we become locked into a world system of multinational corporations and new forms of control and domination.

Unless we regain control of our economy, the work of changing and humanizing our productive system cannot begin. It should be made clear, therefore, why we should strive for that control. The main purpose in regaining control of the economy is not simply to replace American instrumentalists with Canadian instrumentalists, but rather to break the domination of instrumentality over our lives. In order to bring this about, we must be prepared to submerge our productive system within a much broader network of social, cultural and political relationships in which the demands of production will no longer dominate, but instead, production will be planned and coordinated within the context of a much wider range of concerns than simply profit and survival. Obviously this is not possible if our economy is controlled by narrow self-seeking corporations more concerned about their executives and shareholders in New York than they are about workers in Hamilton or local communities in Edmonton. Foreign, private control over our productive system must be replaced by domestic, social control so that we ourselves have the power to ensure that production will no longer have a life of its own but instead will be used to further human goals and considerations.

For Canadians, the second key to breaking the domination of technique lies in integrating the economic potential of the different regions of Canada with the nature and interests of the communities within those regions. Any attempt to return to the simple, frontier type of community on a mass basis would undoubtedly prove futile, since most Canadians would not accept the drastic drop in living standards which such a change would involve. Instead, community and economic development must be tied together in such a way that people can live more complete lives, yet simultaneously be assured of a reasonable level of material comfort. Rather than have large corporations come into local areas, devastate the environment in order to exploit resources, send away most of the profits and then leave, it should be left to people within the region to decide the general level and course of development, consistent with the needs of the community. In this way, communities could be assured of the economic base they need to survive while exercising the type of social control which is necessary to prevent the excesses of the developmental process. In addition, regional communities in one part of Canada could work out the necessary types of exchanges of goods and services with other communities on a much more equal basis, thereby breaking the present metropolitan-hinterland relationship which typifies most inter-regional exchanges in Canada.

Under present circumstances, regional autonomy and self-determination are extremely difficult to achieve because shortages of capital, labour and machinery deter the individual regions from choosing their own course. Part of the blame for this lies with our present federal system which operates merely in terms of compromise between the centralizers in Ottawa and the autonomists in the provinces, providing little direction for Canada and overcoming neither the real nor the relative deprivations of the poorer regions. Rather than continuing to operate our federal institutions on this "balance" principle, the federal system should be integrated with the concept of regional community development. The main role for Ottawa should be that of helping to coordinate the activities of the different regions, but more as a catalyst than as a political body attempting to protect its own power base. In addition, the federal government should use its economic power to assist regional communities to finance developments of their own choosing by borrowing money on world markets, and by raising and re-distributing capital domestically. The federal government should not be regarded as the centre of power in Canada, but rather as a servant of the regional communities, subordinate to their collective wills, and justified only in terms of how it can assist the people in those communities to improve their lives.

Under such a highly decentralized system both provincial and local governments would be expected to play a much more active role in the process of development. Before this can occur, however, people must demand that these structures exercise much greater ownership and control of the resources and indus-tries within their jurisdictions. This process is already under way in western Canada, but in general, most economic power throughout Canada still resides with private corporations, and it will require considerable amounts of effort and capital to bring it under community control. Such control is especially critical in the resource field, because of both the non-renewable nature of many resources and the effect which the development process has on local environments. Without such control, it becomes virtually impossible for people to influence the rate and type of development in their region, and hence they cannot plan and protect the future of their community. In the area of secondary industry, such control is not as crucial to the future of the com-munity, but there are still many decisions involving the location and growth of manufacturing industries which are very impor-tant and which, at a minimum, should be decided jointly by in-dustry, government and the affected community.

In view of the recent takeovers of foreign-owned assets by governments in the developing nations, many of the multi-national resource companies operating in Canada are becoming increasingly apprehensive. Some are threatening to forgo new investments here unless they are given strong assurances that government will not drastically interfere with their Canadian operations. Naturally such a hands-off policy would seriously impede any attempt to integrate development with community interests. In the face of such threats, therefore, provincial gov-ernments should now turn to provincial crown corporations as the main instrument for developing resources. Given the present world shortages, such institutions would have little difficulty in borrowing funds on world money markets to finance future developments, or even in convincing Canadians to invest in such profitable ventures.

As we begin to integrate the productive system with a much broader range of interests and structures, we must also work towards changing the process of institutional domination of the person which has developed with the growth of the technological society. As we have sought to manage society more efficiently, greater numbers of people have come under the control of the corporation, the welfare state, the mental health state and even the police state. Today this entire process is growing geometrically as both bureaucratic and human concerns are used to bury people in bureaucratic structures typified by order, conformity and obedience. Particularly insidious are the legitimate human concerns such as equality and health, which are used to convince people to give up control of their minds and bodies in exchange for becoming either "healthy," "better off" or "good citizens." Under present circumstances, this massive invasion of the person has no limits and can only lead to a degree of control and depersonalization which would shock even the tough-minded George Orwell.

The most immediate results of the growth of "concerned bureaucracy" are the wide gaps of power that have been opened between workers, students, patients and prisoners on the one side, and managers, administrators, doctors and jailers on the other. Controllers and other "experts" are now being granted greater and greater power in the belief that they know what is "best" for us and should, therefore, have the capacity to act on us and for us. Not only do these groups enjoy tremendous power, but they also know how to protect it against those who may question their positions, by branding their critics as radicals, Marxists, Conservatives or trouble-makers, by denying them positions in the structures, and even by diagnosing them as sick people who require treatment to make them "normal."

In order to free ourselves from the increasing power of concerned bureaucracy, we must begin the process of changing the way institutions regard people, and encourage much greater participation in decision-making by those most affected by the controls of these structures. Decisions must be made in such a way that people not only feel that they have some control over the structures, but actually exercise some real degree of power over them. In the productive system, for example, workers should be given a much greater voice in determining wages and working conditions, as well as some say over the general direction of the firm or industry. Without such power, workers will remain merely wage earners, alienated both from themselves and from their product, lulled until the day of their retirement by marginal increments and future pensions. In this regard, the present system of workers' control in Yugoslavia provides an example of how workers can become more than mere employees, although the application of the general concept to Canadian industry could well take different structural forms.

In educational and other social institutions, the present hierarchical system must also be modified drastically or even done away with entirely. Individuals who must interact with these structures should no longer be treated in terms of roles, but rather as sensitive people, aware of their own problems and capabilities, who would not attempt to destroy themselves and the rest of society if given some degree of power over themselves and the structures. In education, this means that students should be considered the equals of faculty and administrators in structural questions, and in intellectual matters should be given much greater freedom to define and answer questions for themselves. In most medical and other social welfare institutions, the mystique of the expert must be abolished as the basis for treating or otherwise dealing with people. Doctors, nurses, social workers and other such types are not gods, and have no right to go beyond the most direct forms of assistance in attempting to help people. The vast systems of surveillance and control now being constructed by these people and their institutions are completely unjustified and constitute a genuine threat to all who come under their power. Doctors, for example, should be treated the same way we treat a plumber hired to fix a leaky toilet: as a sensitive person performing a limited service.

Many aspects of our legal and security systems must also be reformed if these structures are to be genuine agencies of justice, instead of mere methods of exercising control by imposing law and order on those who come into conflict with the present system. Our system of courts, police and prisons must not be allowed to become tools of those who wish to maintain the technological society, but instead must be integrated with the community as a whole. Laws must be formulated and administered on the basis of aware community standards, and police power, in particular, must not be permitted to become a force unto itself, but rather must always be subservient to the will of the community. In addition, the current proliferation of private security agencies, which are designed primarily to protect private corporate interests, must be checked drastically if it is not to become a significant threat to popular democracy. Finally, our system of jails and prisons must be reformed and humanized so that those who transgress community standards can come back into society as more complete persons rather than as bitter, hardened criminals who regard the legal system as simply a way of suppressing the lower classes.

Unless we soon begin to change the entire system of controls which we have constructed over ourselves and our society, these controls will be used continually and to an ever greater degree to support the domination of technique and make the process of liberating ourselves that much more difficult. If we can achieve an alternative to the technological society by developing human cooperation through communal structures and values, then the future of Canada could well hold a broad range of human possibilities. If we fail, then the future may see the end of Canada and of Canadians.

NOTES

1. By essence, Heidegger means the "basis of the inner possibility of whatever is accepted in the first place and generally admitted as 'known'." See "On the Essence of Truth," in *Existence and Being* (Chicago: Henry Regnery Company, 1949), p. 303.
2. Quoted by Herbert Marcuse in *One-Dimensional Man* (Boston: Beacon Press, 1970), pp. 153, 154.

3. Martin Heidegger, *Holzwege* (Frankfurt: Klostermann, 1950), p. 266*ff.*, and *Vortrage und Aufsatze* (Pfullingen: Gunther Neske, 1954), pp. 22, 29.

4. The development of the postulate that nature is objective arose primarily through the work of Galileo and Descartes, who, in formulating the principle of inertia, laid the groundwork not only for mechanics but for the epistemology of modern science, by abolishing Aristotelian physics and cosmology. See Jacques Monod, *Chance and Necessity* (New York: Vintage Books, 1972), p. 21.

5. David Landes, *The Unbound Prometheus* (New York: Cambridge University Press, 1970), p. 1.

6. Peter Mathias, *The First Industrial Nation* (London: Methuen and Co., 1971), p. 4.

7. Ibid., p. 4.

8. Landes, *Unbound Prometheus*, p. 37.

9. See Harold Innis, *The Fur Trade in Canada* (Toronto: University of Toronto Press, 1970) for a discussion of how the Indians were used in the fur trade and then discarded as technically obsolete once the fur trade declined.

10. It is important to remember that there has always been a significant overlap between government and business elites throughout Canadian history which has contributed to the process of economic development.

11. H. C. Pentland, "The Role of Capital in Canadian Economic Development before 1875," *Canadian Journal of Economics and Political Science* Vol. XVI, No. 4 (November 1950), p. 466.

12. The census of 1871 shows that 51 per cent of the working population of the colonies were either farmers, lumbermen or fishermen, 13 per cent in manufacturing and crafts, 18 per cent in construction and unskilled labour, and 18 per cent in services. See *The Rowell/Sirois Report, Book I*, edited by Donald Smiley (Toronto: McClelland and Stewart, 1963), p. 15.

13. R. T. Naylor, "The Rise and Fall of the Third Commercial Empire of the St. Lawrence," in *Capitalism and the National Question in Canada,* edited by Gary Teeple (Toronto: University of Toronto Press, 1972), p. 6.

14. See *The Rowell/Sirois Report, Book I*, p. 23.

15. Donald Creighton, *John A. Macdonald: The Young Politician* (Toronto: Macmillan, 1968), p. 361.

16. Ibid., quoted by Creighton from the *Globe,* 21 September, 1864.

17. Harold Innis, *Essays in Canadian Economic History,* edited by Mary Q. Innis (Toronto: University of Toronto Press, 1969), p. 209.

18. W. A. Mackintosh, *The Economic Background of Dominion-Provincial Relations* (Toronto: McClelland and Stewart, 1964), p. 29.

19. Donald Creighton, *The Old Chieftain* (Toronto: Macmillan, 1968), p. 215.

20. Quoted in *The Rowell/Sirois Report, Book I*, p. 66.

21. See Peter J. George and Ernest H. Oksanen, "Recent Developments in

Quantification of Canadian Economic History," in *Histoire Sociale/ Social History* (Université d'Ottawa and Carleton University, November 1969), p. 78.

22. Melville Watkins, "A New National Policy," in *Agenda 1970: Proposals for a Creative Politics* (Toronto: University of Toronto Press, 1968), p. 160.

23. Ibid., p. 161.

24. Naylor, "Rise and Fall of the Third Empire of the St. Lawrence," pp. 19, 20.

25. Kari Levitt, *Silent Surrender* (Toronto: Macmillan, 1970), p. 64.

26. Herbert Marshall, Frank Southard, and Kenneth Taylor, *Canadian-American Industry, A Study in International Investment* (Toronto: Ryerson Press 1936), p. 3.

27. A. R. Hall, *The Export of Capital from Britain, 1870-1914* (London: Methuen and Co., 1968), p. 1.

28. Contrary to some opinion, northern industry in the U.S. did not, on balance, benefit from the stimulation of Civil War demand. In terms of the arms and equipment used, the Civil War was not a modern war and did not result in a marked increase in the productive capacity of heavy industry, nor did it speed the adoption of new techniques of production. See Lance Davis, Richard Easterlin, William Parker, et al., *American Economic Growth* (New York: Harper and Row, 1972), p. 56.

29. Ernest Mandel, *Europe vs. America* (New York: Modern Reader, 1970), pp. 8, 9.

30. Marshall, Southard and Taylor, *Canadian-American Industry*, pp. 19, 22.

31. Ibid., pp. 36-52.

32. See *Report on Foreign Direct Investment in Canada* (Ottawa: Information Canada, 1972).

33. For a theoretical discussion of multinational corporations, see Stephen Hymer, "The Efficiency (contradictions) of Multi-national Corporations," in *The Multi-national Firm and the Nation State,* edited by Gilles Paquet (Don Mills, Ontario: Collier-Macmillan Canada, 1972), pp. 49-65.

34. Traditional nationalists are particularly concerned with protecting the fate of a people occupying a geographical area by developing an independent nation state through a process of cultural, economic and political integration internally, and by using policies of domestic ownership and control to protect the nation from outside influences. Traditional nationalism demands a high degree of political centralization through a strong national government in order to formulate and enforce the policies necessary to ensure existence as a nation.

35. For further discussion of this point, see particularly Gad Horowitz, *Canadian Labour in Politics* (Toronto: University of Toronto Press, 1968), pp. 1-57.

36. One of the clearest statements of the priority of right to good is found

in John Rawls, *A Theory of Justice* (Cambridge, Massachusetts: Harvard University Press, 1971), especially pp. 3-114.

37. George Grant, *Technology and Empire* (Toronto: Anansi, 1969), p. 19.

38. In the following pages I do not propose a complete plan for Canadian independence and a perfect way of life. Rather, I present some of the structural changes which I believe are necessary to begin challenging the domination of technique and moving us away from our present state of dependency.

39. Here, I am not assuming that the Vietnamese war was fought just to protect American economic interests, for most certainly, the reasons for American involvement were much more complex, but I am referring to it in order to illustrate something of the new relationship between the technological powers and the developing nations which has arisen since the end of World War II.

Nationalism and Communitarianism

There is a rueful European saying which claims that "a nation is a group of persons united by a common error about their ancestry and a common dislike of their neighbours." Canadians, however, have never believed in the common error about their ancestry. The most apparent and outstanding characteristic feature of Canadians remains, to this day, their heterogeneity of ancestry and their diversity of culture, custom, tradition and even language.

If Canada cannot be conceived of as a nation in this first sense, it does, however, appear to be moving towards the self-conception of a nation in the second sense. The common dislike or, more accurately, the dread of our southern neighbour has emerged over the past two centuries as a significant feature of Canadian history. Manifest Destiny, American invasions of Upper and Lower Canada, the Annexation movement in the nineteenth century and the contemporary penetration of the Canadian economy by American-based multinational corporations all attest to the legitimate concern, indeed, pervasive fear, with which many Canadians have viewed historically and continue to view today the American behemoth to their south. The pessimist, of course, might conclude that Canada is only half a nation; the optimist might assert that it is possible to transform this second dimension of nationhood into a positive force, such that by closing the 49th parallel, both economically and culturally, Canadian nationhood can become a reality. In the past few years, this optimistic attitude has assumed the major contemporary perspective on the problem of Canadian nationalism. Today, the debate on nationalism has shifted from the question of the value of preserving the Canadian identity to the more immediate concern with developing specific policies for the preservation and indulgence of this identity.

In recent years it has become increasingly difficult to comprehend, let alone appreciate, the range of concerns associated with the question of Canadian nationalism and the myriad solutions proposed for the final resolution of the problem. Bombarded daily by the appeals of various groups—economic nationalists, continentalists, cultural isolationists, internationalists and separatists—one tends to lose the ability to reflect sensitively and consider thoughtfully the basic character of the question and the nature of the problem. This is especially true today when it is asserted continuously that we live in a totally new situation, the technological age wherein future shock effectively dates our thoughts and sensibilities almost the moment we utter or sense them. We thus confront a double bind: not only is it difficult to comprehend the character of Canadian nationalism itself, but our comprehension must take into account the peculiar patterns of thought and the unique structure of inquiry associated with the technological age.

Given this perplexing state of affairs, one should not desist from undertaking an inquiry into Canadian nationalism. However, it does seem sensible to begin in new terms. In order to appreciate the contemporary and historical character of Canadian nationalism it is first necessary to undertake a morphological inquiry into the meaning of the terms "technology" and "nationalism." The two terms, indeed, share certain similar epistemological roots, and, as a consequence, an inquiry into the meaning of the term technology should clarify certain strands of thought associated with nationalism.

THE TECHNOLOGICAL PERSPECTIVE

Platitudes frequently reveal the basic value of the orientations, attitudes, beliefs, assumptions and preoccupations of an epoch. Today even adolescents flippantly refer to the technological society, the technological age, technological change and so on. This characterization of our era permeates all sectors of our society, from adolescents to the media, from our philosophers to our government. Almost every significant societal institution seems to be imbued with this technological perspective and concerned with its significance for specific public policy.

Throughout the evolution of western thought in the post-medieval era, a particular concern with uniqueness or differentiation has preoccupied thinkers. This preoccupation can be related to the growth of the historical perspective[1] or (as I would prefer to conceive of it) a concern and an obsession with the development of a conceptual apparatus for the purposes of differentiation. During this era, men have adopted a linear historical consciousness and by extending it to the past they have devised the notion of the "contemporary" versus the "historical," the "modern" versus the "ancient," the "past" versus the "present." The philosophic basis of these categories implies an urge to differentiate various periods of human development and enterprise and indicates an impulse to separate the continuity of human effort and activity so that differentiation provides the meaningful basis for understanding. Hence, the term "the technological era" enables us immediately to comprehend other eras, to locate ourselves within history and to identify ourselves with a complex set of ideas that is specifically associated with our era and *not* attributable to others. This conception serves to define our identity, our history and the character of our human activity. In effect, it tells us who we are and how we relate to the past. Indeed, many people would assert that it enables us to relate to the future as well.

Some people claim that the development of this new orientation to man, his history and his place in the world can be related historically to the decline of feudalism and the concomitant emergence of newer forms of social, economic and political structures which later became identified as liberalism. The decline of feudalism can also be understood in intellectual terms as being related to the collapse of Aristotelian science and scholasticism and the concomitant rise of modern science. Indeed, this latter development, which ought to be understood as part of a more complex process of socio-political-economic transformation, also bred the conditions and laid the foundations for the technological perspective.

For the purposes of clarification it is helpful to isolate some of the critical features in the emergence of modern science and the technological perspective. Obviously this emergence entails a vast, complex, historical analysis. However, in many ways Francis Bacon can be conceived as a significant articulator of the major intellectual currents and sensibilities which worked themselves out in subsequent generations and epochs to form this technological perspective.

The genesis of Bacon's thought lies in his articulation of the distinction between traditional philosophy and his desire to establish new foundations for his modern philosophy. In his book, *Novum Organum,* we encounter an articulate statement that the present is and ought to be self-consciously different from the past. Moreover, to Bacon, the critical problem of the modern self-identity revolved around a basic epistemological nexus. He conceived of his fundamental task to be the development of a theory of knowledge which was radically different from previous epistemologies. This point is, indeed, crucial. Whereas other philosophers and thinkers began their philosophic constructions with metaphysics or ethics, Bacon discerned that epistemology must and ought to be the basis for a new philosophic system. If, as I have argued, Bacon articulates the modern, technological perspective accurately, it would seem that the philosophic roots of this perspective reside in a self-consciously constructed epistemological system.

There are four critical dimensions to Bacon's thought which provide significant clues to the character of modern science and the technological orientation.[2] First, he emphasized the importance of research and the communal character of all scientific inquiry. Bacon clearly understood that research was premised upon a "normal scientific" community.[3] He conceived of modern science as a continuous enterprise, encompassing a vast range of particular activities and specialized researchers.

Bacon, however, extended this conception of scientific practice further. He argued that science is a particular and rigorous form of knowledge, one which is based upon a very specific methodology. But this emphasis upon the methodology of science in itself was not novel, for, indeed, Aristotle, Descartes and other thinkers had recognized the importance of method. What distinguishes Bacon and makes him particularly modern and technological was his belief that knowledge was not "to be sought either for pleasure of the mind, or for contention or for superiority to others, or for profit, or fame, or power, or any of these inferior things; but for the benefit and use of life." In effect, knowledge was to be conceived of predominantly in instrumental terms. That is to say, knowledge was an instrument, or tool, in the hands of man, to be used for practical benefits. The validity, importance and worth of knowledge was to be measured in terms of its practical utilities and pragmatic applications and not in terms of enlightenment or virtue. This instrumentalist approach to knowledge clearly links Baconian science to technology. Indeed, this presumption of scientific knowledge as instrumentality provides the epistemological foundations for the technological era. The test of adequate scientific knowledge for Bacon, as for ourselves, relates to instrumental utilities and practical uses, and not to the pleasure of the mind.

The final dimension of Baconian thought which helps define the epistemological foundations for the technological ethos was his belief that knowledge is not only instrumentally useful and beneficial, but also that the acquisition of knowledge in an expansive manner was possible. A particular optimism pervades Bacon's work. If man would devote himself to this communal research enterprise called science in a sufficiently methodical manner, then he could achieve complete knowledge. The full understanding of nature was possible. Furthermore, Bacon claimed that the complete understanding of nature that science pursues would simultaneously lead to the application of this understanding for human purposes. Knowledge of nature, hence, was to be an instrumental knowledge—the commitment to use the knowledge of nature for human projects and human benefit. Moreover, this utilization of nature through scientific knowledge would herald true progress. Progress became both the objective of knowledge and the human ethical imperative. To know more, for Bacon, meant to use that knowledge for practical purposes, which, in turn, meant to live better.

The four critical dimensions of thought outlined above are exceedingly comprehensive, and provide a basis for an understanding of the technological perspective.[4] Science in our modern age is understood as a distinctive method for the pursuit of knowledge which encompasses a communal enterprise of researchers. Scientific knowledge is predominantly conceived in terms of instrumental utilities or, more commonly, technology. Moreover, the modern age possesses a fundamental faith in the coincidence of scientific enterprise with progress and an optimism that knowledge as use is synonymous with living a better life. The parameters of these conceptions not only denote our modern faith; it must also be recognized that these dicta clearly demarcate and differentiate our modern epistemological enterprise from other eras and epistemologies. The conception of knowledge as use is radically different from the Platonic view that knowledge was enlightenment and virtue, or from the natural-law view that knowledge was the comprehension of the eternal order of the world which resides in wisdom.[5]

The integrally close philosophical relationship between modern science and technology has already been noted. What is even more significant, however, is our modern conception that both science and technology are aspects of a new epistemological nexus, both derived from a particular, unique view of the primary role which knowledge plays in human life. In effect, this new nexus replaces both metaphysics and ethics by epistemology as the most critical and important dimension of philosophical inquiry.

In the contemporary technologically oriented world the human imperative is for man to know, and this imperative to knowledge supposedly enables him to use the products of his efforts to live better. In effect we assume that the ethical dimension of life derives from an epistemological imperative. We tend to believe that one of the vital human tasks is "to know"; indeed, we have transformed that belief into an imperative—you ought to know! And because knowing entails using knowledge for practical purposes, coupled with the belief that knowing also entails progress and living better, the epistemological imperative breeds or secretes the ethical imperative. Thus, ethical discourse and the ethical life lose their autonomy. In the technological ethos, ethical imperatives are subsumed as minor features under the independent and primary epistemological imperatives.

The relationship between ethics and epistemology becomes even more complex within this technological perspective. In a world framed within the confines of communal science, instrumental knowledge and the achievement of progress, man assumes a most significant role and place. In such a world, the natural environment is conceived of as an amorphous mass or substance. It can and ought to be manipulated, altered, reconstructed, exploited to meet human designs and purposes. But these designs and purposes are the extension of instrumental knowledge and instrumental knowledge reveals to man a variety of utilities and practicalities. Human design in a technological perspective becomes multi-dimensional, varied. Thus, man must choose. Indeed, choice and possibility become the secondary qualities associated with instrumental knowledge. And because instrumentality secretes an ethical imperative, part of that ethical imperative entails choice. That which is conceived of as ethical in this perspective is the opposite of necessity: it is that which is premised upon instrumental knowledge and choice. Ethical conduct is neither pursuing God's necessary word or will, nor pursuing virtue, because both these criteria entail acting according to necessity in some sense. Without the dimension of choice, ethical conduct in the technological ethos becomes impossible[6] and, further, ethical conduct itself is totally dependent upon the pursuit of instrumental knowledge.

The fundamental optimism and belief in progress which permeate the technological perspective extend themselves into a fundamental faith that man can use his instrumental knowledge to confront any range of problems, pose alternatives and choose among solutions. Man therefore becomes the problem-solver in a world which is filled with open-ended possibilities.

Thus, the notion of living better is inextricably linked to the notion of choice, or decision-making based upon possibilities and options. The greater the range of options, the greater the range of choice and, simultaneously, the better one lives. Human wilfulness becomes the hallmark of ethical conduct in a world organized upon the principles of a technologically conceived epistemological nexus. Man, therefore, assumes the central role in the world. He becomes the designer, executor and creator of knowledge and, consequently, the designer, executor and creator of ethical possibilities.

THE NATIONALISM PERSPECTIVE

An appropriate understanding of our modern notion of nationalism cannot escape from the epistemological nexus I have outlined as the underpinning of the technological perspective. Indeed, the historical development of modern nationalism has been interwoven with the emergence and legitimization of this perspective. Moreover, the outstanding principles of this perspective define and circumscribe the dominant conception of modern nationalism. However, there is another understanding of nationalism which ought to be explored as well in order for us to appreciate the dualistic character of the "nationalism perspective."

For the purposes of clarification, let me distinguish between two different understandings of nationalism. There is the view that nationalism is the set of shared meanings, values and symbols which permeates the articulate or inarticulate consciousness of a given set of people. The critical question in this understanding of nationalism is how do these meanings, values and symbols arise? The response is usually through some notion of organic growth, slow evolution and historical maturation. Shared meanings, values and symbols are characteristic of an organized structure of communitarian life. Communitarian life has a slow evolutionary growth, characteristic of all organisms, whereby extension and development emerge from an original kernel. The outstanding features of the organism are extended and transmitted to newer extensions so that the newer parts are considered part of the natural character of the original organism. When viewed in its totality, the entire organism—original kernel and its organic extensions—are clearly related and, moreover, the newer parts manifest the designs, features and characteristics of the original kernel.

It is both possible and fruitful to view nationalism in terms of this organic analogy. The original kernel can be conceived as some sort of historically fixed emergence of a group or association of people who can be characterized by a given, shared set of meanings, values and symbols. The extension of this original group results from a natural organic extension; the extended group is then perceived as a natural growth, exhibiting all the structural features of the original organism. Indeed, the extended group is indistinguishable, unless by numbers, from the original group. Moreover, growth itself is a slow process of extension and involves an extensive historical time perspective. Nationalism in these terms, therefore, is conceived of as the natural extension of shared meanings, values and symbols from a given group or association of people to their successive generations and the maintenance of the structural characteristics of the original group to its generative descendants. The most common way to refer to this form of nationalism is in terms of the notion of belonging or emotional identification. Persons feel themselves to be part of the structural entity which in any of its historical periods is construed as a structural extension of an original source. Thus, the elements of feeling, belonging and emotional identification characterize this understanding of nationalism.

The critical feature of this view of nationalism is that this feeling, emotional identification or sense of belonging can only emerge from a slow process of organic growth and natural structural extension. This view is closely related to the Aristotelian understanding of the organic quality of community and encompasses a specific concept of historical antecedent and tradition. In terms of this understanding, man cannot wilfully produce nationalism because man cannot wilfully produce organic growth or structural extension. Furthermore, man cannot simply create these feelings, emotional identification or sense of belonging. They occur and emerge through a slow process of accretion and organic development.

Nationalism conceived in these terms can be seen as a very ancient phenomenon. But in the ancient world, this view of nationalism was not associated with our modern notion of the nation state. It was, rather, an attribute of other forms of political, social, economic and juridical human association, like the tribe, the clan, the polis, the city state. The unique features of these forms of human associations were their naturalness, their organic structural qualities and their historical dimensions. Moreover, these human associations proved to be extremely brittle historically. Over a period of decades, if not centuries, they collapsed, through conquest, through dispersion or through non-structural, non-organic extensions. Conquest usually resulted in structural and organic collapse and the dissipation of the organic kernel. The consequence of non-structural, non-organic extension usually resulted in Empire.

The most appropriate term for this view of shared meanings, values and symbols among a given association of people is communitarianism. The critical features of communitarianism—belonging, identification and feeling—relate to people and community, rather than people and nation state. This is a critical point, for in attempting to elucidate the term nationalism, people most often identify the dimensions of communitarianism, but attribute them to the geographic entity we call today the nation state.[7]

The second understanding of nationalism differs radically from the first. In Elie Kedourie's succinct characterization:

Nationalism is a doctrine invented in Europe at the beginning of the 19th century. It pretends to supply a criterion for the determination of the unit of population proper to enjoy a government exclusively its own, for the legitimate exercise of power in the state and for the right organization of a society of states.[8]

According to this view, nationalism is a doctrine, a set of ideas, indeed, an ideology. The specific referent of this doctrine is the modern nation state. The outstanding features of a nation state are: first, its geographic quality or its *territoriality*; second, its *sovereignty,* or the power of the unit of population living within this geographic territory to determine and enjoy its own government; and, finally, the quality of separateness and differentiation from other nation states, or its *independence.* Indeed, territoriality, sovereignty and independence define the character of the modern nation state; and, in turn, these three terms have become identified with the complex of ideas called modern nationalism.

In this characterization of nationalism, two outstanding points should be noted. First, the bases of relatedness among the people living within a nation state are identified primarily in terms of location. And if we conceive of the location of persons to be fortuitous, then the basis of human relatedness is likewise fortuitous. People are members of a particular nation state for no other reason than that they live within its borders as opposed to living within the borders of some other territorially demarcated nation state. The specific powers of sovereignty and independence reside within the territorially demarcated nation state, and the given population who happen to occupy that geographic space, at any given time, exercise those powers. Secondly, in this conception of nationalism, ideas or political doctrines are both crucial and powerful. Extrapolated to the level of ideology, nationalism can be viewed as a belief system[9] of people living within a given territorial unit, the content of which relates to power and distinctiveness.

This second ideational understanding of nationalism is qualitatively different from our previous definition. The essence of the first view is located in the sense of emotional identification, sense of belonging, or feeling that acts as the bond between people and provides the element of continuity between past and present. Thus, the community—the reservoir of this feeling—has a specific historical, organic and structural quality. The second view associates nationalism not with an emotional identification but with a set of ideas relating to power and distinctiveness. The basis of human association in this second view lies in the acceptance, internalization of and belief in these ideas.

As noted previously, the technological perspective induces the belief that all human practices are possible in all realms provided man adopts the correct methods and applies them towards the achievement of his purposes. The confluence and intersection of the ideational understanding of nationalism with the epistemological nexus of technology has resulted in the belief that even nationalism and nation-building can be achieved through the utilization of instrumental knowledge. The only requirement is the development of appropriate instrumental knowledge (commonly called strategies) and its implementation. For example, it is a common belief today that men can, indeed, found new nations[10] or devise strategies for nation-building.[11] This belief not only presupposes the wilfulness of human action and instrumental knowledge applied to nation-building, but it also betrays a fundamental optimism. Many people maintain that modern nationalism can resolve a variety of human problems. Thus, it is commonly proclaimed that it can alleviate poverty, lead to human dignity or, indeed, lead to the promised land. Consequently, nationalism is seen as progressive—a positive feature of the modern world—and modernity itself becomes defined in terms of nationalism, or that complex set of ideas which distinguishes the present from the past.[12]

NATIONALISM IN CANADA

As with most things Canadian, nationalism in this country has been both ambiguous and paradoxical. Its ambiguity emerges from the dual understandings of nationalism I have outlined above. Few people who have engaged in discussions of nationalism in Canada have viewed it in communitarian terms;[13] most have understood nationalism in this country in ideational terms. The paradoxical quality of Canadian nationalism emerges from the fact that nationalism understood in the communitarian sense has been identified with conservatism, or the attempt to maintain the communitarian basis of Canada which extends back to the eighteenth and nineteenth centuries both in English Canada and French Canada; whereas nationalism understood in ideational terms has been associated, overwhelmingly, with liberalism in Canada—that is, the set of political premises and policies which sees conscious, wilful political action as the key to maintaining the territoriality, sovereignty and independence of the Canadian nation state.[14] The historical roots of this second view also reach back into the nineteenth century.

Of these two understandings of nationalism, the ideational one has played a more significant role in framing the character of Canadian public policy. And, indeed, it is no wonder that this is so. If one is a politician committed to public policy, then one must obviously believe in the power of conscious wilful human action and the possibility of achieving practical objectives through the utilization of instrumental knowledge. The communitarian understanding of Canadian nationalism has become less significant in public policy, especially today, when we tend to be ensnarled in the mode of thought and the sensibility of the technological age.

The analysis of Canadian nationalism understood in its ideational conception reveals two primary orientations.[15] The first orientation conceives of Canadian nationalism as the consequence of the sum total of the economic structures and relations in the nation.[16] It is argued that if these structures or relations are dominated or controlled by foreigners, then sovereignty, territoriality and independence are contradicted. This leads to the creation of the conditions for the disintegration of the Canadian nation state. The second orientation conceives of Canadian nationalism in terms of a communication network or the interrelated system of the various manners and modes by which Canadians relate to each other.[17] If this communications network is oriented towards external sources or is dominated by foreign concerns and interests, then Canadian nationalism vanishes as well. Thus, both these orientations lead to the argument that Canadian content and control over either or both the economic structure and the communications network are vital to any conception of a viable Canadian nationality.

These two orientations provide the explanatory parameters for the historical record of Canadian public policy towards nationalism. Indeed, if one examines Canada's national policy historically, one can see clearly the manifestations of these two strategies towards nationalism. In the early years of Confederation, the economic theory of nationalism seemed to be favoured. Hence we had a policy of high tariffs and protectionism. However, since the latter part of the nineteenth century, the communications approach or strategy to Canadian nationalism has become more dominant. Since that period successive Canadian governments have moved to control the diverse forms of communication within our nation—railways, airlines, radio communications, newpapers and television. Further, a concerted attempt has been made to preserve the independence of and sovereign control over insurance and banking institutions.

Today, many people assert that both these orientations and strategies towards nationalism must be extended. Thus, many urge a furthering of the communications strategy—greater control over book publishing, television, radio, cinema and other forms of communications. They argue that Canadian nationalism must be further developed by an extension and intensification of the Canadian content in the media. Others proclaim that nationalism must be furthered through an extension of Canadian control over our economic structures. Hence, they urge the implementation of various forms of Canadian ownership, or effective decision-making power over resources, industry and manufacturing. Without adequate and effective control over the economic structure and/or the communications network, Canadian nationalism will disintegrate.

However, it is critical to note that although the protagonists of these two strategies towards Canadian nationalism tend to view each other as rivals—the latter being identified as socialist-nationalists, and the former as liberal-nationalists—they both share a common set of assumptions. First, independence, sovereignty and territoriality provide the basic philosophic and normative premises for their viewpoints. Secondly, they share a common faith that conscious, wilful, human action can further their nationalist objectives. Their unstated presupposition is that nationalism can be developed, nurtured and effectively encouraged. Finally, they tend to associate the development of nationalism with specific features of this technological age, such as the mass media, corporate finance and industry. In effect, both the socialist and liberal nationalists view nationalism not from different presuppositions, but rather in terms of different strategies for development. It is not the philosophical understanding of nationalism that divides them, but rather strategic considerations.

Canada's experience with nationalism, both historically and in the contemporary age, has been predicated upon these two varieties of technological nationalism. Indeed, one can view the entire development of Canada's national policy as merely the working out in liberal terms of the basic presuppositions of ideational nationalism within a technological ethos, utilizing technologism.[18]

COMMUNITARIAN NATIONALISM IN CANADA

Although technological nationalism has dominated the policy level in Canada and accurately characterizes most of our contemporary orientations towards Canadianization, the communitarian appreciation of Canadian nationalism provides many fascinating clues towards a reinterpretation of the character of a Canadian polity. First, it must be noted that Canada is not a homogenous nation, but rather an assemblage, collection, string or conglomerate of communities.[19] Historically, Canada was populated by the extension of communities, that is, diverse outposts which grew in size, some extending themselves to newer areas, while other regions were settled by communitarian fragments from European countries.[20] The fragmentary growth of the Canadian polity has resulted in significant heterogeneity amongst Canadian communities. The Maritimes, understood as an assemblage of communities, is radically different from Quebec, understood in the same terms, which in turn is vastly different from Ontario and in turn different from the prairies. This basic fact concerning the Canadian political nationality has usually been understood as regionalism. This term, however, does not accurately reflect the historic nor the contemporary character of Canada. The foundations of the Canadian polity rest in communitarianism, and its basic character remains, to today, communitarian, not regional. This critical point implies a host of related factors. First, because of the communitarian foundations of Canada, the notion of the mosaic and ethnicity have remained the most substantial insights into the character of the Canadian polity. Secondly, patriotism to the single nation state, in its naive sense, has been absent in Canada. Instead, Canadians manifest communitarian identities, with vastly divergent life styles, cultures, values and loyalties. The particularistic and fragmentary quality of identities in Canada can best be understood as a reflection of our communitarian foundations. Thirdly, this fact has been reflected continuously on the institutional level in terms of federalism. Canadian federalism ought to be understood in terms of the dynamic tension between technological nationalism, with its urge to create a single independent, sovereign and territorially integral nation, and communitarianism, with its emphasis upon particularism and fragmentation. Most people have naively interpreted this tension as the centralism-versus-decentralism controversy.

The manifestations and ramifications of this basic tension in the Canadian polity help explain other paradoxical features associated with Canadian politics: the rise of third parties which express the communitarian urge of populations; the continued failure of integrationists in Canada; the assertion of provincial autonomy, not only by Quebec, but by other provinces who seek to maintain their particularisms; the continued viability of ethnicity in Canada; the failure of consensus politics; and the difficulties in developing a national trade union movement.

If the Canadian political nationality ought to be understood in communitarian terms, what can the term communitarian nationalism mean? Is not the term communitarianism antithetical to nationalism? If one understands nationalism solely in ideational terms, then, indeed, it is antithetical to communitarianism. However, nationalism understood in terms of the first meaning I have enumerated is quite reconcilable to communitarianism. Communitarian nationalism connotes an assemblage of diverse human communities circumscribed by a given state. The modern nation state must be viewed as a fairly recent historical development whose origins and subsequent development are closely related to the technological perspective. Thus, the term communitarian nationalism highlights the paradox of the historical notion of human community as it relates to and sur-

vives within the technological nation state. The basic philosophical premises of communitarian nationalism are antithetical to technological nationalism. Whereas the latter defines politics in terms of wilful human action, or decision-making and
power, the former presupposes the necessity of diverse human associational development within an historic, organic perspective.
Politics in the communitarian nationalist sense is conceived as
the human activity in which diverse communal purposes are
classified and sought. As opposed to ideational nationalism,
communitarian nationalism would posit that independence is
not a virtue in itself, but becomes meaningful only when it is
supplemented by associational relatedness within the communitarian context. Sovereignty becomes significant only if it implies the acceptance of and respect for the heterogeneity of
human communities. Territoriality, in communitarian nationalism, is not defined simply in spatial terms, but rather is conceived as the complex task of searching for and achieving the
bases of human communal relatedness.

The historical impetus of technological nationalism is towards internal homogeneity within the spatial referent of the
nation state. Distinctiveness and differentiation in this conception relate to some external source—another nation state—as
well as to the discontinuity of history. In terms of technological
nationalism, the notion of citizenship rests upon these two
dimensions of distinctiveness. Thus, Canadian citizens think of
themselves as neither American nor British, and usually assert
their difference from the French, Scots, English, Irish, who came
to this country in previous centuries. There is a further ethical
dimension involved in this conception of citizenship. One ought
to assert one's nationalism and citizenship by developing new
things—flags, anthems, songs, cities, towns—thus affirming historical discontinuity and reconfirming one's identity *vis-à-vis*
some external referent.

Communitarian nationalism, conversely, implies heterogeneity and lodges distinctiveness within and between communities. Rather than asserting historical discontinuity, it stresses
historical continuity, organic development and structural extension. The understanding of citizenship does not relate to the

nation state, but presupposes participation in communitarian activity. The ethical imperative becomes not distinctiveness, but communitarian involvement, and the assertion of belonging to human community within historical continuity.

At this point it is important to raise and dispose of the notion that technology *per se* necessitates the homogenization of life and the destruction of communitarianism. This view rests upon the same idealist naivete that confounds and reveals itself in Ellulian thought. Technology as such is neither a thing nor a power.[21] It is rather a complex, an epistemological nexus, which in our contemporary age has become associated with the nation state and ideational nationalism. There is nothing inherent in the "Idea of Technology" which demands the inevitability of ideational nationalism. It is only when we conceive of both technology and nationalism in idealist terms as Ideas, outside and above historical human development, that we can commit the idealist fallacy and assert their inevitability or their power outside the realm of concrete, historical, human experience. When we examine the concrete historical situation in Canada, for example, we can witness and comprehend the manner in which the technological perespective and the ideational notion of nationalism have emerged and affected the character of public policy.

The contradiction between the historical character of Canadian public policy and the historical foundations of the Canadian political community now becomes apparent. The former has been premised upon the precepts of technological nationalism: the epistemological nexus associated with technology merged with the ideational bases of nationalism. The latter reveals the communitarian character of the Canadian polity and induces an alternative understanding of the nature of the Canadian nationality. To this date, technological nationalism has failed to reveal or enhance the communitarian character of the Canadian polity. Thus, if public policy is to be reoriented in this country, it ought to strive for the resolution of the above contradiction in such a way that the historical and contemporary communitarian character of Canada can achieve its self-expression. How can this be achieved?

There appear to be four main features associated with communitarian life in Canada. First, communitarian life has profound historical roots in this country. The Canadian polity emerged from a series of outpost communities which then developed, not into a single, integrated nationality, but rather into a fragmented, particularistic, heterogenous communitarian nationality. This communitarian pattern of development is radically different from the American pattern of frontierism and individualism.[22] Secondly, in Canada communitarianism has always been associated with a pattern of cooperative, interdependent life. The theme of "survival" in Canadian literature reveals this characteristic most poignantly.[23] Thirdly, in virtue of these two preliminary points, change in Canada has been slow and continuous. Communitarianism implies a particular pattern of historic continuity and development by extension. Canada, as has so often been mentioned, does not possess a revolutionary tradition. The dynamic of technological nationalism demands historic discontinuity, revolution, radical change. Communitarian nationalism, alternatively, presupposes and reinforces historic continuity and slow change. Finally, in Canadian communitarianism, most human associations tend to be small and particularistic. This feature manifests itself in such diverse phenomena as ethnicity, religion and trade unionism.

These four features of Canadian communitarianism provide substantive insights into Canada's past historical development and afford the definitive bases for the understanding of the Canadian polity. Public policy in Canada must, therefore, abandon its commitment to technological nationalism and adopt the communitarian orientation. The false presupposition of technological nationalism is that homogeneity is the imperative of the modern age. Furthermore, communitarianism need not imply the balkanization of Canada, as some people fear. Canada's unique nationality resides exactly in its heterogenous communitarian bases. In more specific terms, the problem confronting Canadian policy-makers is devising forms of human relatedness within the framework of community so as to strengthen community, and seeking substantive bases for the relatedness of diverse communities throughout this country. The imperative, therefore, becomes the abandoning of technological nationalism and thinking dialectically in terms of diversity and relatedness whereby communitarianism is preserved, strengthened and developed.[24]

In a country such as Canada with its communitarian base, it is disheartening to witness well-intentioned people attempting to define the Canadian nationality in terms of "our common dislike of our neighbour" or simply in terms of independence, sovereignty and territoriality. The paradox of Canadian nationalism today is that many people continue to think in terms of rueful European expressions rather than in terms of our historical and contemporary communitarian realities. The possibility of creative politics in Canada rests not with European expressions but with the comprehension and extension of our communitarian nationality.

NOTES

1. See, for example, Karl Lowith, *Meaning in History* (Chicago: University of Chicago Press, 1949) and J. B. Bury, *The Idea of Progress* (London: Macmillan, 1921).

2. Herbert Butterfield, among others, concurs with this judgment; see his work, *The Origins of Modern Science, 1300-1800* (New York: Collier, 1962), chapter six.

3. The phrase "normal science" is borrowed from and explored by Thomas J. Kuhn, *The Structure of Scientific Revolutions* (Chicago: University of Chicago Press, 1962).

4. In the attempt to elucidate the term "the technological era," many thinkers have taken up and expanded certain aspects of Baconian thought. Perhaps the most famous example is Jacques Ellul. He extrapolates from Bacon's preoccupation with method as the essence of science to assert that the technological society "is the totality of methods rationally arrived at and having absolute efficiency . . . in every field of human activity. Its characteristics are new; the technique of the present has no common measure with that of the past." (Jacques Ellul, *The Technological Society*, trans. John Wilkinson [New York: Random House, 1964], p. xxv). Here we find two elements of Baconian thought. First, that rationality is synonymous with a commitment to a particular method and its application to the pursuit of knowledge in all spheres of human activity. If man is to pursue true knowledge he must systematically apply the same method to all his knowledge-seeking activities. Secondly, this new method distinguishes the present from the

past; it makes the modern enterprise of knowledge-seeking radically different from previous searches for knowledge. Unfortunately, Ellul's preoccupation with "rationality" and "efficiency" encompasses only two of Bacon's more numerous modern imperatives or dicta.

5. The Harvard University Program on Technology and Society sought to delineate the parameters of the technological ethos. After asserting the all-pervasiveness of the technological ethos in terms of "machines, but also including linguistic and intellectual tools and contemporary analytic and mathematical techniques," Emmanuel Mesthene states, ". . . we define technology as the organization of knowledge for practical purposes. It is in this broader meaning that we can best see the extent and variety of the effects of technology on our institutions and values. Its pervasive influence on our very culture would be unintelligible if technology were understood as no more than hardware." (Emmanuel G. Mesthene, *Symposium: The Role of Technology in Society*, No. 8 of the Harvard Program on Technology and Society reprints 1969, p. 492). Mesthene, like Ellul, assumes one dimension of Baconian thought and transforms that into an assumed complete understanding of the technological era. In many ways both these writers, like many others who have sought to explicate the technological ethos, are no more than footnotes to Bacon.

6. This, of course, has led many people who are ensnarled in the technological perspective to misunderstand, misinterpret and fail to appreciate thinkers like Rousseau and Plato who conceived of ethical conduct in terms of virtue and necessity.

7. If one examines the contemporary literature on community, one finds a basic confusion. The concept of community is conceived of as a sub-group within the nation state. Further, the nation state is sometimes viewed as being composed of many communities, and people tend to be construed as having dual identifications, i.e., with the community and with the nation state, or that communities cannot survive in the modern nation state. I think the dichotomy between community and nation state is a peculiarly modern conception and emerges from the bowels of liberalism and capitalism which demands an extensive open market place. It is not surprising, therefore, that certain theories of society, like anarchism, which criticize liberal capitalism, can conceive of the resurrection of communitarianism.

8. Elie Kedourie, *Nationalism* (London: Hutchinson, 1969), p. 4. This view of nationalism has had a profound impact upon the thought and writing of Pierre Trudeau; see, for example, his *Federalism and the French Canadians* (Toronto: Macmillan, 1968) and *La grève de l'amiante* (Montreal: Editions Cité Libre, 1956).

9. Obviously, I am simplifying the meaning of the term ideology. I am using it in the sense of a belief system, or an integrated and functional set of ideas believed by someone to be true.

10. This particular phrase has been adopted from the plethora of literature emerging from, mainly, American political science. The notion of the founding of new nations is explored by Seymour M. Lipset, *The First New Nation* (New York: Basic Books, 1963) and Louis Hartz, *The Founding of New Societies* (New York: Harcourt Brace, 1964), and has become a major concern in the study of comparative politics.

11. For a discussion of nation-building see Karl Deutsch and W. J. Foltz, eds., *Nation-Building* (New York: Atherton Press, 1963).

12. Nationalism as an ideology of modernity has played a vital role in the politics of so-called developing areas. Among other books, see Robert Rotberg, *The Rise of Nationalism in Central Africa* (Cambridge, Mass.: Harvard University Press, 1965) and Elie Kedourie, *Nationalism.*

13. The most interesting spokesman of this understanding of nationalism in Canada has been George Grant, in his *Lament for a Nation* (Toronto: McClelland and Stewart, 1965) and *Technology and Empire* (Toronto: Anansi, 1969).

14. I am using the terms conservatism and liberalism to denote movements in the history of political thought and not as rubrics for political parties. It is significant, however, that one can comprehend the past policies of the Conservative party (and later the Progressive Conservative party) and the Liberal party as resting, in part, upon these two divergent views of nationalism.

15. These two orientations are explored and exposed in Peter Russell, ed., *Nationalism in Canada* (Toronto: McGraw-Hill, 1966) and Ian Lumsden, ed., *Close the 49th Parallel* (Toronto: University of Toronto Press, 1970).

16. This argument has a very obvious Marxist basis. It is, therefore, comprehensible why many socialist-oriented thinkers and politicians have adopted this orientation towards the understanding of Canadian nationalism. See, for example, the work of Melville Watkins, Edward Broadbent and Jim Laxer, among others.

17. Karl Deutsch, in *Nationalism and Social Communications* (New York: Wiley, 1953) exposes in great depth the premises and consequences of this view of nationalism.

18. By technologism I mean the faith in the power of technology and the unquestioned belief that technology can resolve human problems.

19. S. D. Clark, among others, in *The Developing Canadian Community* (Toronto: University of Toronto Press, 1962) provides the foundations for this assertion.

20. The fragment theory of the Canadian nationality has been explored in the work of Louis Hartz, in his *The Liberal Tradition in America* (New York: Harcourt Brace, 1955), and *The Founding of New Societies,* and extended in Gad Horowitz, *Canadian Labour and Politics* (Toronto: University of Toronto Press, 1968). Unfortunately, the analysis of Canadian society in "fragment" terms has been restricted to the

ideological dimension of Canadian party politics, and has not been extended to its logical conclusion, which is an historic overview of the development and character of the Canadian nationality.

21. I find that most general discussions on technology tend to reveal an idealistic bias. I fully admit the power, insight and ingenuity of Jacques Ellui's massive work in *The Technological Society*. However, his work betrays a basic philosophical orientation which can best be called idealism. If one treats terms such as technology as Ideas, then one can impute to technology a power independent of human experience and conceive of it as Hegelian-like Spirit. I thing that technologism has become the contemporary form of Hegelianism.

22. Jean Charles Falardeau in "The Seventeenth-Century Parish in French Canada," in Marcel Rioux and Yves Martin, eds., *French-Canadian Society* (Toronto: McClelland and Stewart, 1964), explores the unique communitarian pattern of rural settlement in Quebec. I would maintain that this explanation provides a profound insight into the pattern of settlement in other parts of Canada. Indeed, this explanation ought to be applied to an understanding of the character of urban Canada as well. The recent emergence of community action groups in urban Canada reflects the resurrection of communitarianism.

23. See, for example, Margaret Atwood, *Survival* (Toronto: Anansi, 1972). In many ways Canadian literature is the best guide for an understanding of the communitarian bases of the Canadian polity. Canadian novels tend to relate to persona in small communities and not to persona within an overarching Canadian nationalism. It is no wonder, therefore, that we do not have "the great Canadian novel." Instead we have Montreal novels, Toronto novels, rural Quebec novels, prairie novels.

24. George Woodcock's plea for the conception of Canada as an "anti-nation" (*Canadian Forum*, April 1972) ought to be conceived as a plea for the resurrection of the communitarian comprehension of the Canadian polity. "Unfortunately, most people tend to view Woodcock's vision of Canada as anarchistic romanticism. I think that communitarianism—not anarchism—has profound historical roots in Canada. It is the duty of the Canadian intellectual community to articulate a communitarian vision of the Canadian polity and to formulate concrete policies to achieve the realization of this vision.

John T. Woods

A Cultural Approach to Canadian Independence

Most Canadians will acknowledge the costliness of their national independence. The subtleties of his scholarship may cloud the academic's eyes, but the man in the street can see clearly that the Canadian border holds back the full tide of American prosperity. On the other hand, he has difficulty picking out what this barrier protects. We are inclined to suspect that, had the Fathers of Confederation failed, we would today be enjoying not only the United States' wealth and power, but much of what we presently have as well.

The question of our independent statehood is always with us because, strung out as we are along the thousands of miles of border, we can never escape the American presence and the fact of a magnificent and flamboyant American statehood. Despite our situation, however, we seem disinclined to examine our own independence seriously. We agonize over internal divisions and what we see as external threats, but rarely get down to a close examination of what our independence provides and how these particular benefits are to be preserved. To list the benefits of our own statehood, we must first have in hand a catalogue of those things which states in general can provide their people.

Three Types of State

The state is set off from other social devices by the fact that it provides the laws, those seams of the social fabric which together define a society's form and contain its lifestyle. By way of its laws, the state both fashions a society and provides the most tangible expression of its character.

Among the state's basic provisions for the society is the delineation of its membership, a broader spectrum than that of citizenship. The members of a society are all those regularly permitted some part in its activities. There appear to be three types when we divide states according to this aspect of their character.[1] For illustrative purposes, at least, these might be thought to typify three eras in human development.

The first type is the blood state. Its adherents regard themselves as being of one family, tribe or "race", and seek to exclude others from whatever benefits membership in their society bestows. We usually think of this form as typifying the earliest communities, and whether or not this is historically accurate, it is fair to say that the blood state is the most primitive on a scale of cultural evolution, because it is rooted in something akin to instinct.[2]

The second type might be called the "strategic" or "territorial" state. Once again, most of us are rightly or wrongly inclined to associate this form with an era, most frequently Europe's Middle Ages, a time when territory, together with its inhabitants, was carved up according to the relative strengths of rulers, rather than along the tribal lines of more primitive times. Its purpose was to maintain the position and further the aims of those who controlled it. Its societal members, those sharing in its benefits, however minimally, were simply the people found within its momentary boundaries.

The third type characterizes both our own and classical times. It is the state based on a culture or way of life. Just as Athens and Sparta were distinguished by their distinctive ways of coming to grips with life, so the states of the post-Renaissance era, at least ostensibly, set out to pursue an identified lifestyle rather than to further either the cause of race or the competitive advantage of those within their borders.

There is a fundamental difference between the first two principles of statehood and this last. The first two dictate the formation of societies through a choice of persons, while the last makes a choice of actions, which is one definition of lifestyle or culture. The racial state chooses those of a given genetic inheritance; the strategic state those on the near side of the border. The ideal nation state, on the other hand, admits anyone to the society who is willing and able to deal with life in the chosen way. The clearest examples are the revolutionary constitutionalist states, notably the United States. It is a way of life that is set out in the documents of the revolution, among which the Declaration of Independence remains an inspiration to this day. The most cursory examination of the Constitution reveals its essentially cultural character; the United States is pre-eminently a nation state. Canada cannot make the same claim, and it is from this fact that much of our fumbling nationalism follows.

The nation states arose as a political form out of the epoch of humanism. Most simply, humanism can be thought of as faith in, and reverence for, individual human potential. It follows from this belief that human individuals share moral priority over other entities, and from this proposition in turn flow the more specific beliefs and practices which, while not unique to them, stand out as the signal characteristics of the nation states: democracy, equality, legal equity and so on. Whatever particular formulas and ideologies may from time to time emerge in expression of this premise, the nation state is a means to the end of individual fulfilment, where the term embraces each human individual. But individual human potential unfolds only in hospitable social settings, and belief in the nation state thus tends to carry with it the conviction that the individual's personality, his own repertoire of life-ways, must be consonant with those of the people around him. For instance, where there is conflict, as there will always be, a satisfactory state provides a situation in which the point at issue, together with the terms and the limits of the conflict, are clearly understood by the opponents, and in which the habits they have been provided with by the society constitute appropriate rules for solving it. The society's entire array of rules, be they legal, customary or habitual, constitute culture, the choice of actions. Thus the humanistic revolutions gave rise to the cultural or nation state as an institution.

In practice, every nation state also exhibits the characteristics of both the primitive blood state and that state set up for coldly strategic reasons.[3] There is always some xenophobia, whether or not it finds clear expression in policy, and there is always a strategic element, particularly in the laws concerning economic and financial activities across national borders. To say that pure types are rare is not to say that people prefer it that way, however. The premises of the blood state and the strategic state conflict profoundly with those of the nation state. And the attempt to develop a viable society around such a combination of conflicting premises is bound to be frustrating at both the level of societal order and that of personal tranquility. An individual carrying conflict within his own personality is, by definition, neurotic. We are at peace to the extent that we can resolve such philosophic conflicts.

Cultural Coherence

A publicly viable and personally satisfactory culture is above all coherent. It is a plan for living in which each thought and action is consonant with contiguous ones.[4] Thus, as the arbiter, the state must husband cultural coherence.

Canada, as a small state awash in foreign influences, confronts a chronic question of cultural coherence. The most fundamental aspect of the question is whether or not there is an independent nation here—a cultural unit—or whether the criterion of cultural coherence really makes it part of American society. No two people are exactly alike in personality, no two families in their customs, and no two communities in their norms. How big should a nation state be? How does one identify a sufficient difference in lifestyle between people to warrant making each group sovereign in its independence from the other? If the aim is to maximize cultural coherence, then a nation should be hived off wherever the cost in cultural disarray occasioned by participation in some larger society would be greater than the various penalties attendant upon separation.

Politically speaking, a nation state should be formed wherever a thoroughly aware people feel the need of separation more than they feel averse to its costs. To what extent, then, do Canadians have a sense of their cultural uniqueness, and how much is its maintenance worth to them?

Canada's formation was more a strategically than a culturally inspired act. Driving the railway through from the old union of Canada to both coasts was aimed at preserving the lands of British North America from the growing power of the United States. In the age of the nation state, the ambitions which lay behind the monumental project of Confederation tended to be voiced more in cultural than in economic terms, but it is clear that the quest for economic and political advantage of the people immediately around Macdonald was at least as much a factor as the desire to give political expression to some sense of common lifestyle. The question then arises, is Canada *today* a culturally based nation state, or still a strategic aggregation with some of the trappings of a nation state?[5] If the latter, its legitimacy comes into question.

Certainly, we have never declared ourselves to have a defined way of life, or a national purpose such as bespeaks a common view of it; and, unlike so many of the modern nations, we have undergone no dramatic moment of self-realization. We have not ourselves experienced the humanistic revolution. However, one's nationality need not be conspicuous. First of all, in political terms, the common law tradition of English-speaking Canada is rooted in the assumption of cultural coherence. It works only where people share life-ways. British colonists carrying it with them continued to live here according to British ways. There is no need to make a declaration of principles whose universal acceptance can be assumed, while the inevitable incompleteness of such a statement would render it a source of confusion where informed intuition had previously provided clarity.

The same argument cannot be advanced regarding French-speaking Canada, but its history attests to its cultural coherence. Unlike English Canada, Quebec has, until recently, been relatively free of immigration and the cultural diversity it has entailed for the rest of Canada and the United States. Consequently, Quebec has been primarily an off-shoot of pre-revolutionary France and seen little cultural disruption until recently.[6]

Both sections, then, are internally coherent, but the English-speaking section has never asserted this, and French-speaking Canada has been inclined to confine itself to asserting its distinctiveness from the rest of Canada. Consequently, we remain in doubt as to our nation statehood.

The Canadian Identity

Certain characteristic propositions about life and how to live it are at the heart of any culture and serve to set it apart from others, to furnish the core of its identity. If a society's culture differs in these fundamentals from those of surrounding societies, the differences can be counted substantial and it should be safe to assume that they warrant the costs of independence. Whether or not there is a "Canadian identity," then, a set of fundamental orientations which characterize us is a measure of whether we should persevere in maintaining our independence.

There is substantial evidence that we do have this kind of identity. The importance of the community, particularly the ethnic community, in both our personal and public lives is the most striking of an array of characteristics which together indicate a distinctive orientation toward life.

John Porter's thesis of the "vertical" ethnic mosaic provides a particularly important discussion.[7] He holds that it has been in the interests of a "charter group" of British immigrants and United Empire Loyalists and their descendants to maintain distinctions between the ethnic communities of Canada so as to preserve their own role of leadership. The outcome has been to perpetuate the ethnic particularities of the groups which have come together in Canada. Few would applaud the intent, of course, but we remain at home with the realities of social hierarchies and the peculiarities of people who live in tight communities.

The Porter thesis about how Canada is structured can be supported with historical evidence. The modern phase of Canada's history, a period during which it was beginning to take shape as a politically and economically self-sustaining country, was the most lively period of the second British Empire. British colonization from home had not worked well, judging by the example of the American Revolution, and the emphasis had, to some extent, swung from settlement to trade and investment. Consequently, the second British Empire was built, more than the first, around arrangements with local elites. It was in the interests of the British to employ the leverage of indigenous control, and they promoted those elements of internal stability which did not threaten their supremacy. Tribal coherence was encouraged so long as it did not give rise to strategically significant aggregations of indigenous groups. The British authorities thus became used to thinking of the colonies in terms of interethnic relations, with the English group in control. British protection was thus provided for ethnic *groups,* rather than primarily for individuals.[8]

This policy paid well for some time, and doubtless confirmed the colonizers in this way of looking at social life. In Canada, Durham's proposal for assimilation of French Canada was probably turned down in some part because it conflicted with the assumptions of this view. A far tidier way to handle French Canada was to let it function as a semi-autonomous but subordinate segment of the British North American empire. Britain could then enjoy the strategic advantages of dominion over Lower Canada without suffering the expense or disruption attendant upon forcing its inhabitants to adopt British ways. Later waves of immigration into Canada tended to be handled in a similar spirit, through transplantation of European communities beleaguered by change or disorder there. Canadian or British agencies viewed these people as communal units rather than as individuals, and saw their capabilities and peculiarities in these aggregate terms (at that time "racial" terms).[9] Communities of immigrants were placed wherever in the economy and geography of Canada it was felt they would function best as a community and contribute most.

Another approach to a somewhat similar endpoint is the "Laurentian hypothesis" ascribed to a number of Canadian historians.[10] The American frontier was settled by individuals and groups advancing across the country from east to west by dint of hard, often improvised, and largely individual efforts to settle a land which was wild but not basically inhospitable. Canada, on the other hand, was settled through the early establishment of a series of trading outposts which had to be supported through the harsh winters by colonial authorities, and which were permanently linked by vital but fragile trade routes to a home base in England, France or the St. Lawrence valley. This pattern is by no means obliterated today, at least on the prairies. There is still a feeling that the centre is somewhere else—Ontario, say, or even the United States. Particularly in western Canada, settlement was underwritten by powerful elements of the home community. The settlers were agents of an already constituted authority. Their dependence upon it and their obligations toward it were part of the Canadian cultural heritage from the outset. The outposts grew into hunting and agricultural and, finally, industrial communities. They expanded by way of increasing the range of activities carried on in each. By contrast, the American pattern was to proliferate settlements rather than to develop each one. Once again, then, Canadian history emphasized the role of a community and of a settled, rather hierarchical order in Canadian lives and helped to confirm the accompanying attitudes in the developing culture.

Work in Canadian ideologies suggests similar conclusions about our outlook. The American historian, Louis Hartz, has theorized that the Revolutionary War isolated the United States from the European mainstream of western thought. He maintains that, as a consequence, the American lifestyle has been an elaboration of the early puritanical liberalism on which several of the thirteen colonies were based. In this view, the United States today vests responsibility for both success and salvation almost entirely in the individual, and the community is simply a setting for the exercise of individual initiative rather than an expression of some common fate or purpose. Each man has no intermediary save Christ between himself and God. Each stands alone on a plane with all others.

Gad Horowitz applies similar thinking to the Canadian case. He maintains that because Canada, in contrast to the United

States, was not cut off from Europe, it retains a more complete catalogue of European cultural materials. Rather freely interpreted, Horowitz's work suggests that Canada benefits not only from the rudimentary liberalism of the eighteenth century, but also from the French Catholic and British Tory themes of devotion to the sacred and secular communities and faith in salvation through grace as well as works. There was a correspondingly easy acceptance of hierarchy. Later British colonists, and most particularly the United Empire Loyalists, brought more of the same cultural material, as well as their American liberal notions.

In the eyes of a variety of observers, then, Canada retains the cultural potentials of the modern European dialectic: the communal versus the individual; the hierarchical versus the equalitarian; the worldly versus the other-worldly.

Important differences in people's attitudes toward their communities and political processes follow upon these historical events. Americans are led to assume that people are equally equipped for living except in moral virtue, most particularly in the diligence which is thought to determine each one's attainment. Relative attainment in turn justifies the regard in which each is held. In principle, then, the system is one of unqualified competition between deemed equals.

The impossible moral standards of America's lingering puritanism and the patent inequalities of economic liberalism as we find it in practice drive people to shelter themselves in a measured cynicism. Thus protected, they can take part in their community's life, but, isolated by competition and suspicion from each other, they make their contribution in the only way which this situation leaves open to them, the fervent pursuit of ever-greater production and its more visible corollary, consumption.

Inner-worldly religions such as puritanical Protestantism sanctify inner-worldly institutions, most frequently high political office. The American presidency is a case in point. Its incumbent is wrapped in an aura of sanctity. This effect is heightened by the paradox of leadership among equals. The president is above the run of men by virtue of his office, yet categorically their equal. This appears to be rationalized by making the president, who cannot be a better man, more than a man. He acquires some of the incomprehensibility of the divine. He is removed from conventional human intercourse, and must simply be followed as an act of faith, unless he clearly breaks faith, in which case he is not so much replaced as cast out.[11] To those who are able to see him as simply human, he must appear as a fraud and a blasphemer; this cannot but contribute to cynicism.

One can conclude from all of this that Canada should be both more communitarian and more at ease with the facts of leadership than is the United States.

George Grant builds a thesis on the culture of Canada around what he calls the "primal" encounter.[12] Like Hartz, he directs his attention to the way a society forms its fundamental outlook. His argument, though somewhat less specific regarding cultural substance than that of Horowitz, follows the same general lines. European adventurers and immigrants came face to face with Canada's rugged geography and forbidding climate. The array of old cultural premises with which they were equipped had to be brought to bear on the new situation, and a lifestyle had to be fashioned from them. Thus Grant would doubtless agree that the polarities of our European philosophic heritage remain at the heart of our culture today.

Such research findings as there are on the Canadian culture today, particularly as it differs from that of the United States, support these expectations.[13] Canadians are more immersed in their communities and less intent on their careers; they are more aware of the various old-world heritages than are the Americans; they are less concerned with this world; and they are more at ease than are Americans with the mundane facts of leadership, social rank and personal eccentricity which violate naive liberal notions of "equality."

My own impressions of growing up in a middle-class family of British background in Winnipeg are that the Canadian mentality differs from the American mentality much as these historical, sociological and ideological analyses seem to agree they do. Porter's description of the "vertical" Canadian ethnic mosaic strikes the Winnipegger as a particularly apt description of western Canada as it was during the first half of this century. Here, more than in any place in Canada at the time, the community-centred rural culture of post-feudal Europe lingered and was nurtured. Not only were European peasant communities lifted up and dropped almost intact into waiting positions in the prairie economy, but they were collectively assigned stations in life by the British-nurtured "charter group" who already controlled Winnipeg, Edmonton and the other prairie cities. The prairies supported a society almost of estates, or castes, socially and geographically sequestered on the ample plains.

The case of the Ukrainians is most striking. They were encouraged to work the marginal lands to the north of the best wheat and ranching country, it being assumed that the simplicity and tenacity of "these sturdy people"—judged to be a kind of racial characteristic—suited them (and would suit their children in perpetuity) to the difficulties, primitive conditions and meagre rewards of working the sour soils of Manitoba's interlake district. An often subtle but unmistakable and pervasive pressure was exerted to keep them in the status, first, of peasants and then, with the growth of the cities, of labourers.

The Jews were expected to stay with light manufacturing and merchandising. Their intrusion into the worlds of finance, or the residential districts of the Grain Exchange's and the Manitoba clubs' Anglo-Saxon members, was blocked in any way that conscience would permit; and, on occasion, conscience could be rather lenient in the matter.

The French-speaking Catholics, living almost exclusively in St. Boniface, across the Red River from the city of Winnipeg, were expected to take on labouring but, more particularly, the clerical jobs befitting what was thought to be an inordinate concern with things spiritual and an accompanying lack of business acumen.

Even the genuinely liberal among those of British heritage accepted racist beliefs without qualm and, into the 1950s, people of various ethnic backgrounds spoke of their ancestral homes as "the old country," identifying themselves with it as their cultural home, and having little concern to hasten their assimilation into any Canadian cultural mainstream, however great their identification with Canada might have been in other regards. Consequently, the maintenance of ethnic particularities *itself* became a basic cultural characteristic of the people descendent from these various ethnic groups.

Much of western Canada was settled at a time when there was already a small, stable, optimistic, diligent and wealthy, if closed, elite. Transportation, finances and technology favoured en masse colonizations. The constraints on jobs, and on geographic and social mobility of the incoming ethnic groups, were balanced against comparatively adequate circumstances by their old standards.

The ethnic communities appear to have remained stable long enough to become a continuing part of the cultural process on the prairies, but the forces which helped keep them together have declined sharply in recent years. North America's liberal ideals have had their effects. Education, and standards of performance rather than of birthright, put members of the various ethnic groups on a par. Much of the most westerly portions, particularly the ranchlands of Alberta, seem to have developed culturally more along the lines of the American frontier than along those of the older trade and transportation centres such as Winnipeg. Old resentments and the illusions of ascriptive status do hang on, but, objectively, the ethnic hierarchy was crumbling in the 1950s, and 1960s. What remains is ethnic identification, further associated with the settlements which earlier served as the hubs of ethnic enclaves.

THE THREAT TO CULTURE

Both reading and personal experience, which squares well with it, convince me that there are fundamental cultural characteristics—a "Canadian identity"—setting us off sufficiently to warrant our independence. The question next arises as to just what it is that so many Canadians feel threatens our way of life. How might our culture be disrupted by the presence of the American-based multinational corporation, to take the most frequently raised fear?

At this point, a note of caution is in order. The principle of the culture state does not stand alone at the root of our ideas about the nation. Despite their disruptive effects, the more primitive premises of the strategic and blood states obviously remain. To rationalize the consequent conflicts in our thinking, we introduce false assumptions, with unfortunate results for our actions.

A case in point is the automatic identification in many minds of the multinational corporation with a perceived "American imperialism." This is occasioned by confusion between the threat to cultural coherence posed by the corporation as an alien and powerful agent of socialization, and the strategic threat it poses to individual Canadians with whom it competes. Their retention of strategic-state premises leads people to see this second threat as also directed toward the state, rather than as one confined to legitimate competition between business interests.

But we also believe a strategic threat to the state comes only from some other state, not from a business corporation. To close the ring, we must assume that the United States, as a state, is threatening us. As citizens of a nation state, however, the threat we fear from some other state is destruction of our way of life. It follows that the United States is bent on destroying our culture, as well as devouring our economy. Hence our belief in American imperialism. There may be a potential case against the United States, but such muddled thinking precludes the analysis on which it would have to be based.

Although it is happily uncommon, we have an even more striking tendency to transform our disquiet over the impact of American ways on Canadian life into dislike of Americans as people. On the face of it, there should be no such connection, but, by way of suitable rationalizations, our proper concern that this nation's public and private decisions be dictated by our own desires and skills, rather than those of American corporations or government, is readily put in service of the inclination to discredit those who are not of the blood.

There is, none the less, a serious danger to cultural coherence posed by the American presence. First, the multinational corporation poses a threat distinct from, and more dangerous than, the inroads it makes on Canadian public and private policy. In cultural terms, there is a competition set up for the workers' philosophic allegiance between the American corporation and Canadian society. Even where legislation and enforcement or corporate policy are not remotely at issue, there are innumerable day-to-day instances of the Canadian employee's being diverted by his dependence on the company from behaviour in line with his sensibilities as a cultural Canadian. A brief reading of *Galt, U.S.A.* should convince the sceptical that this effect is far more than the cultural tic it might at first glance appear to be.[14] Each such instance destroys some part of the worker's dignity and introduces a measure of disarray into the pattern of his life. Because his actions are also part of the total panorama, the Canadian lifestyle is to that extent rendered incoherent.

This process appears to be one of the things which most offend and frighten people about the American presence. Given the enormous extent of American ownership in the Canadian economy, we have all had at least a brush with it at some time or other, if only by way of news reports, and it is easy to conjure up a picture of the entire nation, seduced or coerced by the corporations' economic strength and the threat of American strategic presence, to the extent that our own way of living is entirely submerged and destroyed. However, the greater long-run danger is not in the direct effects of such cultural affronts, but in the learning which follows from them.

Confronted by the corporate world's power and well aware of the benefits it can bestow, the person facing its cultural demands may find his life, on balance, more comfortable if he adopts the attitudes it represents, discounting those of his private life as a Canadian. When this happens, a more far-reaching cultural impact is in the offing. Now the original effects of cultural seduction are redirected against everyone whom the convert regularly contacts, and the real cultural assault is under way. To the extent that others depend on him in any way, they are inclined to adopt his attitudes, and the cultural disruption thus spreads through the human networks of the society, each new convert becoming another agent for its diffusion. It is not, then, the first-hand affront of having to accommodate a foreign will, but the pattern of learning which may follow that demands our concern, and this learning will take place only when it is well rewarded. The solution, then, lies in the direction of countering the leverage which these rewards provide.

Foreign-controlled media obviously have a potential for widespread disruption, but, once again, only insofar as people learn from what they see or hear. If a message is totally alien it will not be accepted and, as a message at least, can have no effect whatsoever. If it is intelligible but essentially out of keeping with the lifestyle, it will have no immediate effect beyond a passing confusion or irritation. If, however, it holds out rewards which are valued within the already existing lifestyle, people may take up the favoured suggestions and thus also adopt those elements of the message which are alien and potentially disruptive. If a Canadian youth likes the sound of an American popular song, for instance, he may more readily come to accept whatever philosophic postures it represents. These could be profoundly in conflict with the corresponding Canadian positions.

The same holds for consumer products, such as the American style of transportation embodied in their private, heavy, spacious, fast and highly styled automobile. It may have things about it which are distasteful to a Canadian but, if it is satisfactory on balance, we will put up with its disadvantages and eventually even stop seeing them as such, because they are associated with the satisfactions we experience.

The vast majority of people anywhere, whatever the specifics of their culture, are gratified by success, material comfort, a tolerable workload and well-filled "leisure," all at the forefront of the cosmopolitan industrial lifestyle centred in the United States. In the face of such attractions, we need a way to sort out for adoption those things which can be integrated into our lifestyle at a tolerable cost in cultural incoherence, while rejecting those which cannot.

The High-Leverage Solutions

We will want to use the most effective means we can bring to bear in this task of cultural filtration. In practice to date, however, we have had a tendency to fix our attention on countering the culturally objectionable experience itself, without due regard for the far more penetrating effects which can follow.

The low-leverage solutions are as obvious as the low-leverage problems they are designed to combat, and just as inclined to mask more significant processes. If we were prepared to accept the economic penalties entailed, we could fairly easily devise legislation to prevent American firms overriding the effects of existing Canadian laws on their Canadian subsidiaries, for instance. We could place controls on capital flow into Canada or even nationalize foreign-controlled corporations. If thorough enough, such intervention could alleviate the distress of those caught between what, as Canadians, they think best and what, as members of the work world, they find expedient. It would not be a good way to block disruptive cultural diffusion, however. To ensure against the learning effects, we would have to isolate every Canadian from outside influences, because attitudes spread as readily from one point as from many, albeit more slowly overall.

Canadian media laws have had some culturally beneficial side effects, but they also appear to be conceived as a low-leverage response aimed at protecting us from each potentially offensive message.

We see a vaguely defined problem in American television programming, for instance, and move to block as much of it as we think prudent without regard to the relative effects of different programs. If we were really serious about the cultural effects, we would at least try to block those materials which, despite their potential for disruption, are attractive enough to be learned. Aside from the difficulty of implementing such a policy, however, this procedure would make the fact of censorship more apparent than it now is, and more effective censorship is that much more detestable. In any event, the media laws are intended primarily to increase the Canadian content rather than to diminish the American contribution and, in so doing, they appear to have enhanced the perceived legitimacy of Canadian materials; this is all to the good, since it intensifies our sense that there is a Canadian cultural substance. However, one suspects that a primary impetus for media content restrictions is strategic rather than cultural; that it is intended to provide the Canadian performer a competitive edge for his own sake, not for that of the Canadian way of life.

What we require is not better censorship, whether in the workplace, the marketplace or in our leisure hours. Rather, we must have thicker cultural skins. The high-leverage solutions, those affording greater effect for a given level of intervention, would equip individual Canadians to cope with the cultural assaults upon them and their peace of mind. We should each be able to select and make part of our own personalities those components of culture which will enhance life in the Canadian setting, while rejecting those elements which would diminish it.

If we knew just how to do it, we could assure cultural coherence by providing ourselves with the right upbringing.[15] We could build a base of attitudes and beliefs, both integral and well anchored in whatever intrinsic characteristics we have as Canadians.[16] A person so prepared would be able to savour whatever pleasures his lifestyle provides and, if it were a full, satisfying life, he would not easily be drawn into the gulf of contradictions and personal confusions between his own and some other culture.

To achieve this condition by way of a formal social technology, we would need a more complete map of our culture than we presently have, and we would have to understand more clearly than we do what constitutes a satisfactory lifestyle and how people learn it. We could then present the rules of our lifestyle to each succeeding generation in the optimum sequence and manner, so that each of us would carry about the complete cultural map, as a coherent, well-integrated part of his own well-ordered personality. Although we have no such technology, we do have an intuitive appreciation of these things, and one part of every culture is just such a set of rules by which it is pruned and passed on to subsequent generations. A task presently before us, then, is to refine these beliefs and practices as best we can.

However, even assuming we could achieve complete success by intervening to change family practices and formal education, we would still not have done the service we might by adjusting the culture *itself* to accomplish the same ends. Intervention on the scale required to adjust educational practices may be less gross than censorship of later experiences, but it smacks of the same thing and, while it does offer a higher order of leverage, it is, in turn, far less elegant than acting directly upon rules of living would be. If our understanding of our own culture were sufficient to provide such things as a school curriculum keyed to the need for personal resiliency, then we should also have a fair idea of our cultural dynamics—the patterns of change and potential change—as well as of its static patterns. With this knowledge in hand, we could trigger those particular changes in the culture which would thenceforth *automatically* bring education and upbringing into line with the need for the personal cultural resiliency. This would achieve the same end at the cost of a bare minimum of tinkering with the curriculum and propagandizing parents on the need to bring up their children in specified ways.

The Canadian Identity as Its Own Defence

One approach to such cultural change is available. We know that simple awareness of one's separateness as a person is basic to personality formation. The notions we have about ourselves as individuals anchor each of us in our social surroundings. They are organizing principles, and we draw the rest of the rules which comprise our personalities from the culture in accordance with the dictates of these basics. If, then, a person growing up in Canada, the United States, France or wherever, has among his fundamental assumptions about himself the understanding that he is Canadian, American or French, he will tend to pick up those traits which he encounters under the corresponding labels, those which other people appear to regard as Canadian, American or French, respectively.

On the face of it, then, simply making much of the "Canadian identity" could be a far more fruitful tactic than its detractors believe. For people thoroughly aware of their Canadianness—whatever it is in substance—those things presented as Canadian would be accepted as models of behaviour, however rarely they were encountered. The amounts of foreign-made regulations, products or entertainment to which Canadians might be subjected would matter little if this rule were to hold. We would indulge only those experiences and adopt only those ways which we could view as compatible with the picture we held of ourselves as Canadian.

One of the classic examples of how identity generally affects personality formation comes out of the work of anthropologist, Gregory Bateson.[17] Doing his field work, Bateson faced the question of why males and females respectively, in an isolated and intimate tribal group, could develop widely different patterns of behaviour. Where were their examples? Children of both sexes were daily presented with strong, presumably attractive, models of behaviour from members of both sexes, those of the opposite sex displaying very different patterns of behaviour from what they would themselves exhibit as adults. Bateson's explanation was that people of each sex, once recognizing themselves as such, assumed that their own actions should be different from those having the contrary sexual identity. And, in that these assumptions are shared by members of both sexes, the different actions of members of the other sex are seen to be appropriate for them, encouraged and finally confirmed in them as personality. In this way, two groups of individuals who consider themselves different from each other will draw out and encourage behaviour in each other which really *is* different, so that the anticipated differences are eventually realized. Once such a pattern of behaviour has been set up, our personalities tend to grow by accretion, by adopting those additional elements which seem to us to fit with the way we already are, even though we are not explicitly trained in them by the people around us. The key to identity is simply awareness of identity, conscious or otherwise. Once this is established, the unique personalities each emerge from the welter of possibilities available.

At least at first glance, it follows that if a person sees himself as Canadian, he will adopt the characteristics he thinks of as Canadian. An obvious problem with this is that the "Canadian identity" tags are missing from much of our cultural substance because we have never gone through the revolutionary exercise of defining ourselves. But merely raising the question again, particularly in the present situation of stress and nationalist sensitivity, may well trigger the process of affixing these labels.

More importantly, though, there is a big difference between

the cultural anchoring power of sexual and national identification. Sex is always a powerful force in our lives and it is clear that commensurately powerful identifying characteristics will build up around it. National identity varies in its importance with the seriousness of threat to the nation. In wartime, virtually everything depends on preserving the nation, and national identification becomes a paramount organizing principle for the people. One of the great questions today, of course, is whether there is much of value to Canadians which depends on preserving the nation. If not, then the cultural anchoring power of the Canadian identity is slight; in this case, however, it would also follow that there is no particularly good reason to be concerned about preserving Canada. If Canada were not culturally distinct, the game would already have been lost and there would be scant reason to defend it. Certainly we must not allow the exponents of strategic or blood nationalism to drum up fancied threats so as to heighten the anchoring power of the Canadian identity to their own narrow advantage.

Community and Ideology

The question follows, what important values really are associated with the Canadian identity? Knowing them, we might hope to secure the culture against disruption by consciously centring our notions of Canadian identity in these things, by appending the missing cultural identity tags to them.

Although we are far from having a cultural inventory in hand we do have strong indications, as argued above, that community is peculiarly important to the Canadian way. Consciously building a notion of identity around the communitarian nature of our country might give it sufficient force to make this a basis for cultural consolidation. How this is to be brought about is the next question. A partial answer follows from contemporary ideological trends.

At the present time there is a fundamental shift in the axis of ideological debate under way in the developed industrial world. From an opposition of the worker to the owner and the public to the private sector, the central organizing concern is shifting to the more classic question of the public versus the private life.[18] The public life of technology, organization, production and ostentatious consumption stands at one pole. At the other we are beginning to see clearly a revival of concern for aspects of humanism which have not been salient in recent decades, a dual emphasis on wholeness of the human personality and the deeply social character of the species. From this reawakening follows the impetus to contain the productive process in its entirety, to reassert the primacy of the human community over the mere means which have brought it to its present level of wealth and apparent security.

At present, however, the working ideological postures of the industrial world remain much as they have been. Formal political debate must be cast in those terms which are intelligible to the people: private versus public enterprise, East versus West, all to a significant extent surrogates for the fundamental polarity of production, the worker versus the manager. Generally speaking, the people of the industrial world have not yet recognized the societal and ideological trends present in their midst sufficiently to deal with the new realities, to devise, or even respond politically to, the ideas and terms in which these realities must be portrayed.

Canada, however, has never been totally committed to the conventional polarities of liberal democracy. The pre-revolutionary elements of our heritage do provide better for the classical view. We are inclined to see people in their wholeness rather than in their several capacities as producer-consumers—as complex members of complex communal organisms rather than as the occupants of roles in the mass-productive order. We also tend to be aware of the dichotomy between these two views.

The individual and his community are critical to our ways of thinking. The place of industry within the community has been a classic question, and the emergence of a new ideological axis aligned with our habits of thought may well provide the key to maintaining our cultural coherence. It will give us a set of terms and symbols permitting us to raise communal attitudes and assumptions to the level of explicitly stated beliefs, concerns and aims, thus sharpening our dull sense of national identity. Furthermore, a political realignment along the new axis of the public life of production-consumption versus the private life of the human community would bring a classic, pivotal question of Canadian national politics back into the open. Will Canada be as it is represented in the emerging myth of John A. Macdonald and the CPR—a separate community won by the sacrifice of sheer profitability in favour of community solidarity —or will we accept the primacy of industry over nation—the North-South over the East-West axis—and see the nation, if not the state, ultimately dissolved? Were the issue joined we might end by allowing the nation to slip away. But this should not happen by default, and present ideological trends do hold out the promise of a forum in which to deliberate the essentials of the question.

The National and the Local Community

If the communitarian thread is sufficiently strong in our make-up to serve as an organizing principle of a coherent and robust Canadian culture, we must take seriously the diversity of the local communities which comprise the larger one of Canada as a whole. From its earliest times, Canada has been federal in the broader sense that it has bound widely dispersed settlements to a common political community.

One way to enhance the local community's anchoring power is to promote the independence of these many communal segments. But any such policy would have to be accompanied by another designed to ensure that we retain a strong sense of the continuity between our smaller communities and that of Canada as a whole. In the setting of such complementary policies, local identity becomes national by extension.

Perceived disjunctions, on the other hand, visions of the community as separated from the national entity, subject people to an enervating cycle of confusion, fear and hostility. If it is impossible for a man to say, "I am a 'Québécois' " in one breath, and "I am a Canadian" in the next, he must for the sake of his tranquillity give up one or the other idea about himself. The longer he carries this contradiction about in his mind the more deeply he will be confused and irresolute, the less evenhandedly he will be able to manage his life and the less worth living it will be. If he does choose to see himself as a metropolitan Canadian, he becomes a stranger in his own community; if he renounces the Canadian element in his view of himself, he also revokes his loyalty to his nation state, and in an international order still based on competition between nation states this is dangerous indeed. More immediately, he remains bound to the nation state which he now regards as alien.

How, then, can one increase each constituent community's cultural robustness and at the same time maintain Canada? As a first approximation, at any rate, the answer is obvious, and we have been trying to apply it since the fall of New France: it is the principle of the *federal bargain*. Loosely put, each community must be given the power to pursue its own peculiar ends in so far as this will not impair the pursuit of the nation's common purpose. But as it stands today, the federal bargain is at best a questionable deal between regions and at worst the framework for a contest between an Ontario-based coalition of politicians and those from the regions which are left out. We need a much more culturally rooted and genuine federal bargain and one fundamentally broader in scope, distributing powers as far down the line of diminishing governmental size as feasible. Only in this way will people be able to see that their local styles and purposes are supported by national action, that their local identities are compatible with national loyalties, and that their local communities are truly parts of Canada.

Just how this cooperation might be achieved in the face of the many contrary pressures is no small question, of course, but it will not be answered before it is properly put. Some of the tactics are reasonably obvious. Cities, for instance, should be given the power to control their physical surroundings, bringing them into line with the character and situation of the people in the community. For this, the cities will require not only a deeper tax base but a broader one, freeing them from the plan-destroying need to boost property values at every opportunity for the sake of higher property-tax revenues.

For regions, such a revitalized federal spirit should dictate extensive local control of regional economies. Prairie banks, Quebec's control of its industrial financing, schools and welfare systems may well strengthen the national bonds in the final analysis and actually enhance rather than diminish federal authority, because people will be able to see that local and central purposes are compatible and embrace both levels in one identity.

Conclusions

If all the changes I have suggested could be implemented and if we nonetheless failed to halt the trend toward cultural "homogenization", as George Grant calls it, we could fairly assume that the Canadian lifestyle was already so close to that of some U.S.-based, cosmopolitan industrialism that Canadians are ready to take it up with no significant cost to them in cultural disruption. If one further takes the position that the only acceptable nationalism is that of cultural coherence, we should, in the event, let Canada fade away as a focus of our loyalty. It would have been demonstrated that Canada serves no useful purpose.

Whether the test will take place is moot, however. The cultural engineering I have suggested depends largely on a technology we do not yet possess and political circumstances which do not yet obtain. But this does not absolve us from the duty to try, and ordering our thoughts on the problem at least suggests avenues to be explored.

BIBLIOGRAPHY

Bateson, Gregory. *Naven.* 2nd ed. Stanford, California: Stanford University Press, 1958.

Barnett, Homer G. *Innovation, the Basis of Cultural Change.* New York: McGraw-Hill, 1953.

Becker, Howard. *Through Values to Social Interpretation.* Durham, N.C.: 1950.

Cook, Ramsay. *The Maple Leaf Forever.* Toronto: Macmillan of Canada, 1971.

Daniels, Roy. "Literature Part I," in Julian Park, ed. *The Culture of Contemporary Canada.* Ithaca, N.Y.: Cornell University Press, 1957, pp. 1-80.

Deutsch, Karl W. *Nationalism and Social Communication: An Inquiry into the Foundations of Nationality.* Cambridge, Mass.: M.I.T. Press, 1953.

Emerson, Rupert. *From Empire to Nation.* Cambridge, Mass.: Harvard University Press, 1962.

Festinger, Leon. *Conflict, Decision and Dissonance*. Stanford, California: Stanford University Press, 1964.

Grant, George. *Lament for a Nation: The Defeat of Canadian Nationalism*. Toronto: McClelland and Stewart, 1965.

Grant, George. *Technology and Empire: Perspectives on North America*. Toronto: House of Anansi, 1969.

Haber, Robert A. "The End of Ideology as Ideology," in Chaim L. Waxman, *The End of Ideology Debate*. New York: Simon & Schuster, 1968, pp. 182-205.

Hartz, Louis, ed. *The Founding of New Societies*. Toronto: Longmans, 1964.

Hayes, Carlton J. H. *Nationalism: A Religion*. New York: Macmillan, 1960.

Hudson, Liam. *Frames of Mind*. London: Methuen, 1968.

Innis, H. A. "Economic Trends in Canadian-American Relations," in Harold A. Innis, *Essays in Canadian Economic History* (ed. Mary Q. Innis). Toronto: University of Toronto Press, 1956.

"Futurology: Interview with Robert Jungk" in *The Human Context*, Vol. III, No. 1 (March 1971), pp. 182-190. Reprint and translation from 1970 *L'Express* interview.

Kohn, Hans. *The Idea of Nationalism*. New York: Collier Books, 1967. (First published 1944).

Lithwick, H. H. and Paquet, Gilles. "Urban Growth and Regional Contagion," in Lithwick and Paquet, *Urban Studies: A Canadian Perspective*. Toronto: Methuen, 1968.

Lower, A. R. M. *From Colony to Nation*. Toronto: Longmans, 1964.

McPherson, C. B. "The Social Sciences," in Julian, *The Culture of Contemporary Canada*. Ithaca, N.Y.: Cornell University Press, 1957, pp. 181-221.

Mill, John Stuart. *Considerations on Representative Government*. New York: Liberal Arts, 1958. (Original published 1861).

Minogue, L. B. *Nationalism*. New York: Basic Books, 1967.

Morton, W. L. *The Canadian Identity*. Toronto: University of Toronto Press, 1961.

Morton, W. L. *Manitoba, A History*. Toronto: University of Toronto Press, 1957.

Nisbet, Robert E. "The Quest for Community," in *Dialogue*, Vol. 6, No. 4 (1973), pp. 13-21.

Oliver, Edmund H. "Saskatchewan and Alberta: General History," in Adam Shortt and Arthur G. Doughty, eds., *Canada and its Provinces*. Toronto: Glasgow, Brook & Co., 1914, pp. 147-280.

Perry, Robert L. *Galt, U.S.A.* Toronto: MacLean-Hunter, 1971.

Pilisuk, Marc. "Cognitive Balance and Self-Relevant Attitudes." *Journal of Abnormal and Social Psychology*. Vol. 65, No. 2 (1962), pp. 95-103.

Rokeach, Milton. *The Open and Closed Mind*. New York: Basic Books, 1960.

Sahlins, Marshall D. and Service, eds. *Evolution and Culture*. Ann Arbor: University of Michigan Press, 1960.

Sherif, Muzater and Cantril, Hadley. *The Psychology of Ego-Involvements.* New York: John Wiley & Sons, 1947.

Sherif, M. and Carolyn W. *Groups in Harmony and Tension.* New York: Harper, 1953.

Shibutani, Tamotsu and Kwan, Kian M. *Ethnic Stratification: A Comparative Approach.* London: Macmillan, 1965.

Sorokin, Pitirim A. *Social and Cultural Dynamics, Vol. I: Fluctuation of Forms of Art.* New York: The Bedminster Press, 1962.

Spiro, Melford E. "Culture and Personality," in Sills, ed. *International Encyclopedia of the Social Sciences.* New York: Macmillan and The Free Press, 1968, pp. 559-563.

Tawney, B. H. *Religion and the Rise of Capitalism.* London: John Murray, 1926.

Viereck, Peter. *The Unadjusted Man: A New Hero for Americans.* Boston: Beacon Press, 1955.

Wallace, Anthony F. C. *Culture and Personality.* New York: Random House, 1961.

Watson Jr., Thomas J. *A Business and its Beliefs: The Ideas That Helped Build IBM.* Toronto: McGraw-Hill, 1963.

Wiener, Herbert. *The Human Use of Human Beings: Cybernetics and Society.* New York: Doubleday, 1954.

NOTES

1. This paper does not call upon "nationalism" directly in developing the argument. The word is laden with intricate and disparate meanings and is properly a subject for analysis rather than an analytic term. Definitions suggest mixtures of the components discussed here, and my categorization can be considered an attempt to unpack the complex notion of nationalism and estimate its effects on those subject to it as a psycho-social phenomenon. This classic definition of nationality, for instance, suggests a complex of conditions and sentiments such as we tend to associate with nationalism.

   Nationalism comprises: 1) territory; 2) some common culture; 3) some dominant social or economic institutions; 4) independent government; 5) a belief in common history; 6) love of fellow nationals; 7) devotion to the "nation"; 8) common pride in achievements; 9) disregard for or hostility to other, like groups; and 10) hope for a great and glorious future. Listed by Boyd C. Shafer, *Nationalism: Myth and Reality* (New York: Harcourt Brace and World, 1955).

2. Different interpretations are supportable. Consider the following for instance: "As each group develops its own vocabulary of motives, the activities of outsiders become more difficult to anticipate; in some cases their deeds become incomprehensible. This reinforces the conclusion that they are fundamentally different kinds of human beings." Tamotsu Shibutani and Kian M. Kwan. *Ethnic Stratification: A Comparative Approach.* (London: Macmillan, 1965). Once such lines have

formed, the attitudes on both sides tend to become "inflexible, stereo-
typed and projective" as described in Norbert Weiner, *The Human Use
of Human Beings: Cybernetics and Society* (New York: Doubleday, 1954)
p. 281.

3. As in the case of nationalism so in that of nationality, a complex of the
three is generally evident in definitions and descriptions. (Indeed, many
appear to see scant distinction between nationality and nationalism).
Rupert Emerson sees little point in extricating the nation's various
components.

Definitions of the nation which cluster the three bases are common.
Consider Emerson's description of the European ideal of nationality:
"a single people, traditionally fixed on a well-defined territory, speaking the same language and preferably a language all its own, possessing
a distinctive culture and shaped to a common mold by many generations of shared historical experience". Rupert Emerson, *From Empire
to Nation* (Cambridge: Harvard University Press, 1960) p. 96. Mill put
less emphasis on the territorial aspect than some later analysts, but
the complex of cultural unity and personal affinity remains. "A portion
of mankind may be said to constitute a nationality if they are united
among themselves by common sympathies which do not exist between
them and any others—which make them co-operate with each other
more willingly than with other people, desire to be under the same
government, and desire that it should be government by themselves or
a portion of themselves exclusively." John Stuart Mill, *Considerations
on Representative Government* (New York: Liberal Arts Press, 1958),
p. 229. Lewis Mumford sees culture and blood as mutually supportive
rather than conflictual components of nationality. "Those who speak
the language with the right tone and inflection, using the familiar
vocabulary, are kinsmen, neighbors, fellows: people to trust. Those who
do not are outsiders and enemies: at best, ridiculous creatures, not
quite 'people', as the ancient Egyptians openly felt. So the deepest bonds
became in time one of the greatest of barriers between the tribes and
races of man; and man's most universal artifact, the spoken word, because it is so deeply steeped in the individuality of experience, became
an obstacle to the union of mankind." *The Transformations of Man*
(New York: Collier Books, 1956), p. 18.

4. Another definition of nationality illustrates this point, this one by
Karl Deutsch from his *Nationalism and Social Communication: An
Inquiry into the Foundations of Nationality* (Cambridge, Mass.: M.I.T.
Press, 1953) , p. 28. "All these elements—relations to environment, past
leaders, institutions, and symbols—were further shown as making up
structures. They formed configurations, it was urged, in which no single
trait need be as important as the mutually reinforcing and in part self-
sustaining pattern of the whole."

5. George Grant, like John Porter, sees the society built around its economic elite. Can we, then, regard the nation as an economic, hence
strategic entity, an example of "State Capitalism," rather than a

nation state? George Grant, *Lament for a Nation: The Defeat of Canadian Nationalism* (Toronto: McClelland and Stewart, 1965), p. 10.

6. Historians dispute this point, however, and there is a good deal of evidence that many of the attitudes we associate with latter-day liberalism were present, even in the Catholic religion. See, for example, A. R. M. Lower, *From Colony to Nation* (Toronto: Longmans, 1964), especially pp. 25, 32-33.

7. John Porter, *The Vertical Mosaic* (Toronto: University of Toronto Press, 1965).

8. Historians might consider this thesis both crude and presumptuous, but the intent here is to ferret out an essential attitude, not to provide an adequate explanation or appreciation of events; that is properly the historian's role. My impression, upon reading those who have provided such discussions, is that this spirit permeated and directed much of the second empire's politics. Failing this, it was surely at least a constituent of the guiding perspective.

9. There were enterprises set up for the purpose during the settlement of western Canada, where this phenomenon is most marked. An early history recounts, for instance, the conflict between individual frontiersmen and corporately sponsored immigrant communities. ". . . the system of granting immense tracts of the choicest lands to colonization companies was asserted (by [N.W.T.] Council and settlers) to be inimical to the best interests of the country." Edmund H. Oliver, "Saskatchewan and Alberta: General History" in Adam Shortt and Arthur G. Doughty (eds.), *Canada and Its Provinces* (Toronto: Glasgow, Brook & Co., 1914), p. 166. In addition to describing the events, this account itself expresses the attitudes of the time. Immigrants are described, and even pictured in ethnic groups and categories. An illustration opposite p. 176 is captioned: "Types of Immigrants Arriving in Canada 1) Galicians, 2) Russian Jews, 3) Dutch. . . ."

10. Harold Innis and Donald Creighton are perhaps most prominently associated with the school, although many scholars obviously share much of the thesis. Its core is the notion that Canadian development follows from the wedding of mainly European culture and economic capabilities with peculiarly Canadian geographic circumstances.

11. For instance, Theodore White's book on the Watergate scandal is entitled *Breach of Faith*.

12. This term appears in many of his essays but is most fully discussed in *Technology and Empire: Perspectives on North America* (Toronto: Anansi, 1969).

13. See Robert Presthus, *Elite Accommodation in Canadian Politics* (Toronto: Macmillan, 1973), pp. 82-85, for a brief review of findings. Also see, S. M. Lipset, "Revolution and Counter-revolution: The United States and Canada" in Orest Kruhlak, Schultz and Pobihushchy, eds. *The Canadian Political Process* (Toronto: Holt, Rinehart and Winston, 1970), pp. 13-38.

14. Robert L. Perry, *Galt U.S.A.* (Toronto: Maclean-Hunter, 1971).

15. Widespread awareness of our cultural vulnerability—in Canada and in the world—appears to be part of the inspiration behind the emergence of "futurology." See "Futurology: Interview with Robert Jungk," in *The Human Context,* Vol. III, No. 1, (March 1971), pp. 182-90.

16. See Anthony F. C. Wallace, *Culture and Personality* (New York: Random House, 1961), p. 129, for a discussion of the "psychological screen" which excludes incompatible elements.

17. Gregory Bateson, *Naven,* 2nd ed. (Stanford, Calif.: Stanford University Press, 1958).

18. Galbraith observes for instance that "the notion that the individual is all powerful, that the modern corporation is an automaton subordinate to the world, can't survive. It is too drastically in conflict with common sense." From "The Public Purpose of Economics: An Interview with John Kenneth Galbraith," *Dialogue,* Vol. 16, No. 4 (1973), pp. 52-63.

STEPHEN CLARKSON

CANADIAN-AMERICAN RELATIONS: ANTI-NATIONALIST MYTHS AND COLONIAL REALITIES

Why nationalism has been such a negligible force in Canada's recent decades must puzzle any scholar of twentieth-century politics. The country is economically exploited, militarily absorbed and culturally assimilated by the most nationalist of super powers along three thousand miles of frontier. Yet observers who point out that this situation undermines Canada's chances of survival as an independent state are attacked not only on the grounds of being "nationalist" but with the more serious accusation of being "anti-American"—having the effrontery to question the wisdom of the imperial power from whom all blessings are presumed to flow. Canada's economic relationship with the United States is typically colonial, exports consisting mainly of raw materials while imports are mainly manufactured goods. The economy is largely dominated by the corporations from the imperial centre which have also infiltrated all the media of cultural development, turning Canada into both an economic and intellectual hinterland of the American metropolis. However colonial the Canadian-American relationship may appear to the objective observer, it is nevertheless true that the relations between these two countries have been characterized by the most harmonious and amicable attitudes. Despite the disparity of power wielded by the United States, points of tension have been the exception, not the rule. Any hint of a national liberation movement might make sense internally in Quebec *vis-à-vis* Ottawa, but is inconceivable for Canada *vis-à-vis* Washington.

Most attempts to explain this anomaly raise more questions than they answer. A McLuhanesque view which explains the invisibility to Canadians of American dominance by pointing out that the environment is always invisible raises the question why the colonial relationship has been perceived in other dominated countries and why another American neighbour, Mexico, responded to the United States' border presence with a countervailing nationalism rather than a welcoming acceptance. More structural explanations based on such factors as the weak and fragmented nature of the Canadian political system do not explain how other even more divided countries such as India responded to a well-entrenched colonial rule with a lengthy and tenacious independence struggle.

Canada's anomalous relationship with the United States cannot properly be understood without appreciating the basic paradoxes of its historical consciousness, its bureaucratic behaviour and its intellectual culture, factors that have created and perpetuated a political mythology of independence that is clearly out of kilter with the political reality of Canada's dependence.

AN IMPERIAL, NOT COLONIAL CONSCIOUSNESS

While it is often said that Canada has always been a colony, passing from the French to the British empires and from the British to the American system without ever gaining independence, it would be better to understand Canada historically as an outpost of empire, rather than a conquered colony. It was peopled by emigrants from various mother countries, rather than immigrants to a new promised land. As an outpost its economy has from the beginning been created as a hinterland providing a staple—whether beaver pelts, agricultural produce or raw materials—in exchange for the artifacts of civilized life—whether "*les filles du roi,*" access to Oxbridge or the latest gadgets produced by New York's consumer technology. Whatever characteristics Canada's economy may share in common with that of Third World countries, Leninist theory will always fail to grasp that Canada's white dominion colonialism has less in common with the Western-dominated African or Asian societies than with the experience of classical Greece, whose colonies were an extension of the home culture by settlement across the sea rather than by expansion via conquest. If the economic tie with the metropolis is perceived as a beneficial life-line or indispensable umbilical cord then there will be little talk of exploitation. Dependency becomes a continuing reminder of a needed relationship with the metropolitan market for selling beaver and wheat or securing its needed capital and labour for development.

Historically protected from immediate territorial aggression first by the Pax Britannica, then by the Pax Americana, Canada has never experienced any greater threat to its political integrity than an abortive Yankee expedition during the American Revolution, hostilities during the War of 1812 and raids by Fenian terrorists in the 1860s. Nor should one be misled by what might appear as the anti-Americanism of Canada's founding myth. True, the United Empire Loyalists trekked north from the newly independent republic out of reaction against and a flight from the new American democracy. Loyal to their basic imperial tradition as defined by Great Britain, they were replanting their Tory outpost. When the imperial centre shifted from Britain to America it was not difficult for the Canadian outpost mind-set to adapt, both absorbing the Americans' enemy, communism, as the external social threat and accepting American society as its policy archetype. This shift in ideological dependency can be seen as the slow maturation of Canada's national personality, which transferred its infant dependency upon a French parent and childhood attachment to a British guardian into an adolescent enthralment with its richer and more glamorous uncles and cousins to the south. Nothing in the experience of the last generation who fought in the Second World War for King and democracy undermined its imperial consciousness. In the decades since 1930 Canadians have identified any potential international danger as coming from the ideological menace of fascism or communism rather than from any direct territorial threats coming from specific foreign powers such as Germany and the Soviet Union. This sheltered history helps account for the persistence of a white dominion *Weltanschauung* among the overwhelming majority of Anglophone Canadians, a feeling that Canadians form an integral part of the white, English-speaking world community that will only survive by holding together in a troubled globe.

While there were no direct threats that would precipitate a nationalist reaction, nor were there integrative processes at work that could outweigh the centrifugal tendencies rooted in the country's geography and demography. As a country Canada has a relatively small population of twenty-two million people spread thinly across a huge northern territory that spans five and a half time zones covering regions of widely varying levels of economic and social development, the whole being tied together in a loose political federation. In obvious contrast to the United States of America, Canada has no heroic founding myth. For the French population their historical memory is one of conquest by force of British arms. For Canadians of British extraction there is little more than the negative tradition of Confederation precipitated by fear of American expansion. A lowest common denominator of rejection is not a powerful cement to hold ethnically distinct groupings together. On the contrary, internal tensions between Francophone and Anglophone Canada revolve around the very legitimacy of the federal state structure. Whereas the minority Francophone population has a clear historical and social consciousness, the English-Canadian majority demonstrates continuing uncertainty about the historical validity and political integrity of its territory.

The imperial consciousness imbedded in the Canadian psyche was again demonstrated in Canada's first major ventures into world affairs when it responded to the call of imperial mentors in both world wars. Indeed, the golden age of Canada's world involvement was not at all a time of being a dominant loner but as a subordinate team mate, working with superiors, albeit friendly ones, in an alliance of unequal states, holding common goals of collective security.

After these ventures in war, Canada had developed from an

outpost of empire to a key bastion of the Atlantic power system. Since emerging as the world's fourth-strongest country in 1945, it self-consciously devoted itself to the cause for which it thought it had fought the war—collective security. As ideological tensions developed with the Soviet bloc, Canada took a leading role in establishing the North Atlantic Treaty Organization, expected to be more reliable than the United Nations as an instrument of collective defence against the perceived Stalinist threat to the Western world. As it had during the world wars, Canada prided itself on contributing more than its size would call for in materiel and top-quality personnel to the unsung housekeeping work of these organizations. In addition, it helped pioneer the new modalities of world peace, foreign aid through the Colombo Plan and peacekeeping through such supranational operations as the United Nations Emergency Force in the Near East.

While admirable in its moral dimension, this devoted alliancemanship placed an unrealistically high trust in the solidarity of the alliance and made a dangerous assumption about its concrete relevance to the country's basic problems. The public was told idealistically that its foreign policy was not "narrowly nationalistic" but rather internationalist. Canadians were skipping a stage of historical development, showing the world how to transcend considerations of national egoism to embrace the twenty-first century objective of international harmony. This two decades' worth of international effort did have some psychic payoff for Canada. Government leaders and the information media were not reluctant to take pride in Canada's self-effacing do-goodism, an effort given world acknowledgment by Lester Pearson's winning of the Nobel Peace Prize in 1957.

The sad truth, of course, could not be ignored forever. While Pearson's quiet diplomacy might occasionally have been effective, Canada's potential as keeper of the international peace was severely limited. The country's relative power was dramatically declining as the larger states rebuilt their war-torn societies. A white, English-speaking member of a Western military and economic alliance could hardly be welcomed in the councils of the

Third World as if it were non-aligned. In 1967, the year that English Canada discovered some basis for self-pride in its centennial celebrations—the same year, however, when French-Canadian discords were given international recognition with General de Gaulle's *"vive le Québec libre"* cry—Canada fell crashing from its state of international acclaim with Egypt's expulsion of Canadian peacekeeping troops from the Gaza Strip. The Pearson era had apparently left as legacy nothing but a memory of brief glory. Canada could not play its self-appointed role of peacekeeper, it realized, unless this happened to suit not just the super powers' interests but also those of the disputing Third World countries themselves. Although Canadian politicians liked to call the country a "middle power," it was becoming increasingly clear that Canada was declining as a power and was rather better at muddling than mediating.[1] With Britain going into the European Common Market and with France both withdrawing from NATO and attacking the Canadian federation, Canada suddenly found it was playing its international team politics alone. But at the very time that Canada was forced to fall back on its American connection for lack of any other sustaining world relationship, the American imperium had lost its benign appeal to Canadian internationalism and American economic dominance had turned Canada from imperial outpost to colonial appendage.

CONTINENTAL INTEGRATION THROUGH INTERNATIONALIST POLICIES

A second perception of why Canadian nationalism has had such trouble in coming to grips with the meaning of Canada's American relationship can be gained from observing the country's difficulties in generating policies towards the United States. The extent to which the spirit of togetherness has prevented Canadian policy-makers from dealing with the otherness of the United States can be seen most vividly in the processes and product of the foreign policy review initiated by Prime Minister Trudeau in 1968.

Having been under considerable intellectual pressure on the

issue of an independent foreign policy for Canada during the Liberal party's leadership campaign, it was natural for the successor to Lester Pearson to single out foreign relations in his first press conference as prime minister designate to be a policy area needing fundamental review. Following his successful 1968 election campaign run on the slogan of participatory democracy, the public could have been forgiven for expecting that Pierre Trudeau's promised foreign policy review would be open and fundamental. This was not to be. The Department of External Affairs was charged with the responsibility for the review, thus making it judge of the inquiry into its own activities.

The involvement of Canadians in formulating foreign policy bears comparison with the American situation, where academics and politicians move in and out of the State Department as consultants, advisers and ambassadors. In Canada, where the Department of External Affairs, along with the cabinet minister in charge, has enjoyed a virtual monopoly in formulating and communicating foreign policy, there has been no such tradition of elite involvement, quite apart from public participation in foreign policy issues.[2] Modelled explicitly on Britain's foreign service mandarinate and unhampered by a vocal community of academic international relations experts, the Canadian diplomatic establishment had been traditionally free to pursue its internationalist inclinations under the convenient cloak of "quiet diplomacy." As an ideology for diplomats "quiet diplomacy" had been cunningly conceived, claiming to best further Canadian interests behind the closed doors of diplomatic negotiations and to best wield Canadian influence through the quiet application of a credit fund of international goodwill built up so carefully over two decades of persistent effort alongside its natural American, British and European allies. But a strategy whose official rationale of quietness precluded proof of effectiveness (if diplomats told how successful they had been, they would be violating the principle of quietness) was less and less able to satisfy the increasing doubts being voiced about the direction of the country's national development.

The only major voluntary association with serious foreign

policy interests, the Canadian Institute of International Affairs (CIIA), was not structured or staffed to challenge this diplomatic orientation. Originally founded to increase the awareness of the educated public on international issues, CIIA had expanded its activities to embrace some support for research in foreign policy issues. But with the funds coming from the Ford Foundation and ultimate responsibility vested in a board of directors with solid corporate credentials, there was little danger that CIIA's thrust would challenge the Canadian attitude of passivity towards the United States. Thus it was CIIA that was commissioned to organize the selective involvement of the academic community in the government's foreign policy review.

As a result *Foreign Policy for Canadians* was as contemporary in style with its six coloured and easy-to-read brochures as it was traditional in content.[3] The non-nationalist tone is established with the first section, "Canadians as Internationalists." The concern for Canada's role in the world is seen in the review's format: an introductory brochure followed by a separate brochure devoted to each of Europe, Latin America, the Pacific, the United Nations and international development. There was no volume, however, on Canada's foreign policy toward the one dominant force which has a greater impact on Canada than all foreign countries combined—the United States of America. The United States was mentioned, of course, and even rated two page-long subsections, one on "American Impact on Canada's Economy and Other Economic Developments" found in the introductory volume and another on "Growing Concern About American Influence" located in the volume on Europe. The fact that American policy could be relegated to occasional references sown through the text illustrated the failure of the Department of External Affairs to conceptualize Canada's American relationship as being an "external affair" like other bilateral inter-nation relationships.

In the wake of the critical reactions to the document's studied avoidance of Canada's American relationship, the department produced a supplementary brochure on the American relationship. Published just two weeks before the 1972 federal election, "Canada–U.S. Relations: Options for the Future" was intended to meet the country's disenchanted nationalists' concerns. Appearing in the Department of External Affairs' glossy journal, *International Perspectives,* it succeeded less in redefining the issue of Canadian dependence than in confirming how foreign to the federal bureaucratic mind is the language of Canadian nationalism. Whatever acknowledgments of nationalist concern the paper contained were counterbalanced by reversions to outpost-of-empire thinking. The Canadian-American problem was identified as a "vast disparity in power" as is Canada's "profoundly unequal dependence." But no sooner was the wide belief that "the continental pull, especially economic and cultural, has gained momentum" acknowledged than the contrary view was put forward: "it would obviously be absurd to proceed from the assumption that Canada is today substantially deficient in independence."[4] In its policy conclusions the paper recommended "a comprehensive, long-term strategy to develop and strengthen the Canadian economy . . . to reduce the present Canadian vulnerability," though it immediately cautioned that "there is clearly no possibility of our being able to surmount overnight Canada's heavy dependence on the United States for trade, investment and technology." While mouthing the ideas of Canadian nationalists, the document was still speaking in the well-manicured tones of quiet diplomacy: "there is nothing in all this that should be thought to imply a scenario for greater contention." In stressing "the need for the relationship to be harmonious," the Department of External Affairs revealed how inappropriate were diplomatic niceties for the realities of a tough bilateral relationship.

Ottawa might not be able to re-conceptualize the Canadian-American relationship in its old internationalist vocabulary. Even when the American impact on Canada was seen as an internal rather than an external affair, Ottawa had great difficulty in absorbing the message that the American impact on the Canadian economy was not beneficial.

What was remarkable about the role of foreign capital in Canada was not so much the unparallelled extent of foreign control that had been permitted to develop in the Canadian economy and culture as the inability of the political system to respond to this problem. The Canadian economic-development syndrome since the Second World War had been so completely based on American technological values, organizational models and financial sources that information challenging the utility of this process was denied by opinion leaders and rejected by politicians. The Watkins Report, the result of a year-long, government-financed task force study which constituted the first thorough examination of foreign investment and the structure of Canadian industry, was the most obvious example.[5] Published in February 1968 during the final weeks of the Pearson government, the report was tabled: its contents were released to the public, but consideration of its implications by the government was indefinitely postponed. Even when the successor Trudeau regime was installed in office, the Watkins Report lay unattended. No ministry took it up. Even the House of Commons officially ignored it until its standing committee on External Affairs and National Defence decided under the chairmanship of Ian Wahn, M.P., to deal with it in the course of its review of the Canadian-American relationship. But consideration by the parliamentary committee did not mean acceptance by the government. The committee's own findings, the Wahn Report[6], which updated Watkin's information while reaffirming the thrust of his recommendations, was read by the interested public but ignored by the government. The third in this series of reviews was no better fated. Organized once again by a specially designated cabinet minister, the Gray Report was rejected by the government despite the public expectations raised by the inadvertent publication of the major thrust of its analysis which, once again, confirmed the general position taken by the Watkins Report.[7]

This dogged resistance to the overwhelming documentation questioning the value to Canada of being a passive appendage to the American imperial economy is a tribute to the deeply indebted continentalism of the country's bureaucratic structures. That "economic nationalism" was a generally pejorative term used to identify those on the left of the policy spectrum in each political party is a semantic confirmation of the political system's inability to cope with what was a fundamentally different mind-set about Canada and its American relationship. It was not the fact of being a hinterland of an imperial system which was under debate. It was on the value of this situation to Canada that the debate occurred. The United States of America was our best friend and essential world leader for the one group while, for the other, it was the major factor inhibiting an independent Canadian foreign policy and itself the most serious destabilizing force on the world scene. Its role as the major source of capital for investment in Canada plus its position as Canada's major market and chief source of imports was sufficient *raison d'être* for the continentalists and prime cause of concern for the nationalists. Even though Canada was without rival as an "advanced" nation so completely dependent on decisions made by government and business forces outside its borders, so fully integrated in a system of military alliances whose world view it no longer accepted or so completely tied into a self-castrating reliance on imported technology, it was easier for both politicians and public to take its visible power symbols of national flag and what passed as national anthem to be reality, whereas the most dynamic institutions of power in Canada—the American controlled multinational corporation, the American-dominated trade union movement and the American government itself—were not visible to the naked eye and were generally dismissed as only peripheral problems.

That the false consciousness of its internationalist mythology still won out over the reality of its continental and increasingly colonial reality could be seen in the politics of Canada's decision-making on its military alliances. For functional as well as political reasons, military policy has been separated from foreign policy in Canadian public discussion. With a separate department, minister and budget, Canadian defence policy is operationally distinct from external affairs. Since the military establishment touches more Canadians through its troop employment, bases and defence production contracts, defence policies have had a greater salience in the public eye. The program of Defence Minister Paul Hellyer to integrate the three armed forces into one unified armed service provided a major topic for the Canadian public over a period of several years.

More significant for our purposes is the debate over Canada's role in NATO and NORAD which received considerable public attention during the mid 1960s as the deadline for the decennial renewal of the North Atlantic Treaty approached. Although the general issue was Canada's role in military alliances, what is noteworthy about the debate is the extent to which discussions of NATO predominated over discussions of NORAD. The quality and intensity of argument increased in direct proportion to the distance of the controversy from the major issue, dependence on the American military machine. Experts and politicians alike found it easier to discuss the communist threat in the Mediterranean or European weaponry capabilities than to face head-on the implications of Canadian participation in the United States' continental military system. At the hearings of the parliamentary committee on External Affairs and National Defence, members of Parliament frequently asked witnesses for their opinion on whether the United States would retaliate if Canada reduced its commitment to NATO or carried out a de-nuclearization of its forces in North America. It was symptomatic of the real role of the public in making military policy that the NORAD agreement was quietly renewed in the dying weeks of the Pearson government without any debate when Parliament was not sitting and that the Canadian government apparently made no serious representations in Washington concerning the installation of the anti-ballistic missile system. In striking contrast, the extent of Canada's continued symbolic troop commitment in NATO was the subject of extensive public hearings. The publication in the press of some critical articles by intellectuals only underlined the success with which the academic community had been excluded from this decision.

The government's performance has remained consistent in this regard, the white paper on national defence having been prepared with even less attempt to involve the public than the white paper on foreign policy.[8] Whether the far greater Canadian emphasis of this document, which gave the military priority to safeguarding national sovereignty, reflects the growing public concern for national survival or simply a bureaucratic desire to cut Canada's defence coat according to the budgetary cloth was difficult to determine. There was no doubt, however, that Canada's military integration in the continental defence system was to remain unchallenged, whether in the strategic sense of accepting its anti-communist assumptions or in the economic sense of participating through the country's American branch plants in the Pentagon's defence production contracts.

AN ANTI-NATIONALIST INTELLECTUAL TRADITION

The stubborn bureaucratic and political resistance against developing a Canadian-American strategy, whether as a foreign or economic policy, is a clear measure of the low degree of nationalism embraced by Canada's ruling elites. That the independence issue was not dealt with even when it had been identified as highly salient both in the eyes of the media and the mind of the public suggests that there may be a more basic, conceptual issue at stake. If policy-planners are unable to perceive the problem of national dependence, one has to inquire whether their intellectual framework is incompatible with a nationalist consciousness.

Canada would appear to have all the attributes necessary for a national intelligentsia. There are numerous universities across the country with full academic staffs and a student population of some 375,000. An external observer might have expected the natural professional functioning of this intellectual community to have produced a clearly national ideology: Is it not in the Canadian academic community that one should find the nation's intellectual soul? The answer to this question in Canada has been No. For the academic community has itself only very shallow roots in the nation, being largely made up of implants grafted on from abroad. The rapid postwar expansion of the Canadian university, achieved by doubling the number of university campuses across the country in twenty-five years, tripling the number of community colleges and quadrupling the number of students, necessitated not just the hiring of individual scholars but the importing of whole departments. Coinciding with a period of over-production in U.S. graduate schools and a consequent glut on the American faculty market, it was natural that Americans should flood north into these new universities, all the more because of attractive tax exemptions offered visiting faculty and because the expansion of the Canadian graduate schools was still not able to meet the hiring demand. It was not just the new universities which were overrun. The established campuses that had been partially bled of their younger talent to provide the administrative core of the instant college boom were glad to expand their roster of faculty with American names that had some "international" status. Only a minority 38 per cent of the full-time social science professors at Canada's largest campus, the University of Toronto, are Canadian citizens. At the same time a majority—54 per cent—received their last degree in the United States.[9]

The Canadian university had been traditionally apolitical. Modelled on the British tradition that gave a priority to humanities, it had consciously sent its best graduates abroad to be inducted in the professional norms of Oxford or Cambridge, Harvard or Princeton. Only 28 per cent of the social science professors at Ontario universities received their last degree in Canada. Those who returned to the Canadian campus easily integrated into a profession whose career standards were based on esoteric dialogue with their brotherhood of international specialists rather than public communication with the national community. Without a widely distributed intellectual press there were few organs through which the professor concerned about policy issues related to national survival could in fact communicate with his national constituency. Those intellectuals who were non-conformist enough to write on national policy issues did so to the detriment of their academic careers, since books aimed at the general public and not based on continentalist assumptions have not been considered professionally acceptable by academic juries.[10]

While its conditioning militated against any active academic involvement in forming attitudes and making policies on Canada's American relationship, Canada's implant university even failed to develop an academic expertise in what is one of Canada's most intriguing potential areas of intellectual investigation. A familiar set of vicious circles obstructed Canadian-American studies. It is not possible to study the impact of America on Canada if there is no serious literature on the problem. One cannot expect to find a substantial body of literature if there are no academic tools suitable for producing the necessary research.

Even in the disciplines which grapple with problems in their national dimension, the Canadian-American relationship has been traditionally evaded as a subject in its own right, largely because of the way that economists and political scientists define the boundaries for their own disciplines. The professional economist's analytical weapons assume away the political factor. Capital flows, comparative advantages or welfare maximization are notions based on a model of a free market which only grudgingly accepts the reality of the nation state. Economists will gladly discuss whether the auto pact increases efficiency of labour or capital, but will resolutely refuse to be inveigled into considering the power implications of such an industrial merging within the two countries' economies. For their part, political scientists have proven equally reluctant to take on a problem that falls between their stool and that of the economists. The political role of the Canadian branch-plant of an American multinational corporation, or even the different levers used by American politicians, bureaucrats and entrepreneurs to achieve their economic objectives in Canada, are virgin lands for the scholar of Canadian politics. Even within the narrower bounds of what is considered the legitimate domain of political science, the American relationship has never been given serious attention. While the Canadian-American relationship belongs clearly within the sub-discipline of international relations, there has been no foreign policy analysis of this inter-nation dyad that can equal in quality the studies by Canadian historians on past relations between the two countries. Although one could argue that the interpenetration of the two polities is too intense for it to fall within the foreign policy pigeon hole, the practitioners of comparative politics have been equally loath to devote much attention to it. There are specialists and publications on Canadian parliamentary politics and American congressional politics, but they too have defined Canadian-American politics out of their range of concern.

No adequate intellectual tools have been created because there has been little desire to fashion them. That American dominance or Canadian dependency has received negligible research priority is itself a result of the Canadian scholarly community's continentalism. As colonial elites brought up to look first to France, then to Britain and finally now to the United States for their professional finishing schools, it is not surprising that the Canadian universities have been a major force in retarding the country's recognition of its continuing colonization. If the professional norms and career prizes for the Canadian social scientist are set in American graduate schools, if the ground rules of the academic market place are made so as to discriminate by tax exemptions in favour of short-term American teachers wending their career way towards Harvard and Berkeley via the Canadian campus, it is understandable that there has been a general reluctance by the university's faculty to identify the American relationship as a major academic concern. When the conventional wisdom is anti-nationalist, policy-makers cannot be expected to see the nationalist light.

Factors parallel to those causing the university's failure to recognize the Canadian-American relationship have prevented the formation of government policy on Canada's American relations. The politicians' incapacity to deal with Canada's major external problem results largely from the general lack of information that would make this issue visible. The absence of information has been a result of the inadequate sources of data selected by such institutions as Statistics Canada. The failure to develop adequate data-collecting agencies itself resulted from the generally low level of public concern about the problem. The low public priority to questioning the American relationship is, finally, directly related to the politicians' and parties' inability to articulate the problem.

CONCLUSION

If the discrepancy between internationalist myth and continentalist reality is so great, the issue of Canada's survival as a separate political system depends on re-mythologizing its identity. In McLuhan's terms this would require making visible to Canadians the largely unperceived costs of their integration in the American imperium.

Developments over the past decade offer some indication that the level of national consciousness is in the process of shifting. Externally, Canadians have witnessed the decline and fall of the American Dream. The disastrous U.S. involvement in the Vietnam War shattered the assumption that Canada and the United States shared a common world view. The repeated viewing of racial riots and urban degeneration on the nation's television news kept bringing home the message that American society might not be so much the model for Canadians to follow as an example to avoid. Washington's gradual turning of the economic screws on its branch plants abroad kept raising the pressure on Canada. The harsh "Nixonomics" of August 1971 and the subsequent shopping list of American demands on the Canadian economy made it clear to anyone wanting to see that the priorities of the continental economy were: America first, Canada last.

Henry Kissinger is undoubtedly more soothing to the Canadian psyche than was John Connally. Ford is less obnoxious than was Nixon. The new American ambassador to Ottawa can wax eloquent on how our "special relationship" has been replaced by a "unique relationship."[11] But new personalities and new rhetoric are not enough to change the old reality. Even when the energy crisis gave resource-rich Canada an unexpected card with which to improve its own bargaining position, the country's politicians were not able to alter their passive performance. Paradoxically, the most powerful were the most unwilling to stand firm. Peter Lougheed, premier of Alberta, the oil and gas province, and Donald Macdonald, then minister in charge of the energy sector, led the pack of politicians who were themselves being led by the foreign-controlled oil and gas industries. They agreed to Washington's demand that Canada's exports of cheap gas continue; they promised to let the domestic price of oil rise to the artificial level imposed by OPEC and the oil cartel; they even got into bed with the multinationals in developing the Alberta tar sands at maximum expense to the public and minimum risk to the companies.[12]

Neither the reluctant creation of the Canada Development Corporation nor the establishment of the Foreign Investment Review Agency should be seen as a late conversion of Ottawa to the tenets of economic nationalism. As their intellectual god-father, Walter Gordon, put it himself,

I do not think that either of these initiatives amounts to very much. The CDC was launched with considerable reservations and changes from the original concept. FIRA, in my humble opinion, is basically a big joke on the Canadian public.[13]

At the same time, within Canada a process of maturation can be observed, at least among the postwar generation, that is gradually coming into positions of power. The increasing number of graduate students who prefer to do their doctoral research at Canadian rather than foreign universities, the explosion of creativity in the visual and performing arts, the outpouring of Canadian literature both in fiction and non-fiction, all bear witness to an important shift towards a psychic liberation of the intellectual and cultural life of the country. The fundamental strength of the political culture shown in the innovation spreading through the country's municipal structures offers some hope that the political system will gradually respond to the positive nationalism of the country's younger generations.

The spreading consciousness of Canada's neo-colonial exploitation, the awareness of the strait jacket that continental integration imposes on the country's policy-makers and the intellectual self-confidence born of a new celebration of local culture may close the book of Canada's paradoxes. It will still remain to be seen whether the vitality of this new-found maturity will be strong enough to reverse the processes of re-colonization and direct Canada onto a path of self-generating independence in which a redefined nationalism plays a creative and integrating role.

NOTES

1. See J. King Gordon, ed., *Canada's Role as a Middle Power* (Toronto: Canadian Institute of International Affairs, 1966) and my review, "Muddled Views on Middle Powermanship," *International Journal* XXI, No. 3 (summer 1966), pp. 366-70.
2. Franklyn Griffiths, "Opening Up the Policy Process," in Stephen Clarkson, ed., *An Independent Foreign Policy for Canada?* (Toronto: McClelland and Stewart, 1968), pp. 110-18.

3. Department of External Affairs, *Foreign Policy for Canadians* (Ottawa: Queen's Printer, 1970).

4. Mitchell Sharp, "Canada-U.S. Relations: Options for the Future," *International Perspectives* (Autumn 1972), p. 2 *ff.*

5. *Foreign Investment and the Structure of Canadian Industry* (Ottawa: Privy Council Office, 1968).

6. *Eleventh Report of the Standing Committee on External Affairs and National Defence Respecting Canada-U.S. Relations* (Ottawa: Queen's Printer, 1970).

7. "Citizen's Guide to the Herb Gray Report, *Domestic Control of the National Economic Environment*," *Canadian Forum*, Vol. LI, No. 611. (December 1971).

8. *Defence in the 70's* (Ottawa: Queen's Printer, 1971).

9. University of Toronto, *Brief to the Committee on University Affairs*, Government of Ontario, 1971, Table CUA-71-0.

10. An academic review of Kari Levitt's important examination of Canada's branch plant economy, *Silent Surrender*, attacks the work as inadequate scholarship because it is not "predicated on an intensive case study approach" and dismisses it as having only "political significance in Canada." *Canadian Journal of Political Science*, Vol. IV, No. 3 (September 1971), p. 422.

11. Speech by Thomas Enders to the Men's Canadian Club, Ottawa, March 23, 1976.

12. Larry Pratt, *The Tar Sands: Syncrude and the Politics of Oil* (Edmonton: Hurtig, 1976), 197 pages, and James Laxer, *Canada's Energy Crisis* (Toronto: James Lorimer, 1976), pp. 137-72.

13. Letter from Walter L. Gordon to the author, March 19, 1976.

the economic health and stability—a need dictated by the intricate and costly technology employed in the modern corporation. The future of Canadian labour lies in its ability to adjust to these realities, an ability which has not been readily demonstrated in the past.

THE NEW INDUSTRIAL STATE

The central feature of contemporary life is bureaucracy—that vast cobweb of rules and procedures which lays down "rational" grades or levels of accomplishments and orderly prescriptions of conduct as the defined steps for rising or finding a place in the world.[2]

For a century—since Karl Marx delved into the relationships between economic growth, technical change and social institutions—a small minority of economists has actively pursued the organic relationships between technology and institutions. Thorstein Veblen, Adolf Berle and Gardiner Means, Joseph Schumpeter and, most recently, John Kenneth Galbraith, have been the most prominent.[3] Indeed, Galbraith's *New Industrial State* remains the most ambitious synthesis, incorporating recent empirical and theoretical observations. It is within the context of his perception of the new industrial state that our discussion of Canadian labour and technology takes place.[4]

Professor Galbraith has defined the new industrial state in terms of the several hundred "technically dynamic, massively capitalized and highly organized" multinational corporations which dominate the American and Canadian economies.[5] His central thesis relates the development of a complex technology imbedded in physical capital (computers, production line machinery, et cetera) and human capital (education and training) to the nature, size and behaviour of the modern large corporation. Stated simply, the complexities of modern technology require large amounts of capital investment and specialized manpower. Indeed, the decision to invest in capital and in the hiring of a "technostructure" (managers, engineers, designers, market analysts and the host of other highly priced labourers), must be taken months or even years before the corporation's product reaches the market. But to paraphrase the old adage, there is many an uncertainty between the decision, once taken, and the realization of the fruits of that decision, particularly as the elapsed time between decision and realization increases. That means that the greater the time and investment involved in a new production process or new product, the greater the potential economic loss should the market not be receptive or should the prices change markedly during the interval. Therefore, in the Galbraithian model, the modern corporation adopts practices and spawns corporate tentacles quite unlike its classical antecedents, the purpose of which is to reduce the risks during the gestation and life-cycle period of a product or marketing line.

Given these dictates of the modern technology, the modern corporation has adapted. It has resorted to massive advertising to ensure that demand for a specific product materializes when it is finally marketed. It has diversified product lines by branching out into different markets and industries through the mechanism of horizontal integration and the formation of conglomerates, thereby reducing the instability that would result should one product or industry fail. The corporation has attempted to control or circumvent the market for intermediate goods, usually through the mechanism of vertical integration, buying into its suppliers in order to control costs and guarantee steady supplies of necessary material and factor inputs. In the managerial field technical personnel have been co-opted into the decision-making of the corporation by the bureaucratization of the decision-making process. Political adaptation is manifested in support for government policies to regulate and maintain the level of aggregate demand in the economy.[6]

Within the context of this kind of structure and behaviour, the postulate of independence of supply and demand determination, central to traditional economic theory, is untenable. In addition, since the modern corporation will often sacrifice short-run gains for long-run stability and market control, classical textbook models of profit maximization have little meaning. But the institutions of labour, which never fitted well into the static models of economists, may be more meaningfully analysed within this organic frame of reference.

LABOUR IN THE NEW INDUSTRIAL STATE

From the above conception of the corporate system, Galbraith and many others have argued that labour organization has become largely redundant and, in fact, unions have either entered a period of permanent decline or verge on doing so, unless they adopt a new approach and role. The reasons he outlines in some detail.

First, the growth of absentee ownership and the concomitant development of the professional technostructure, the development of intricate and capital-intensive technology, and the regulation of demand and factor supply, all encourage management to attempt to eliminate all potential sources of labour supply insecurity, either through the replacement of labour by machinery or by paying premium incomes for loyalty and continuity. "What the technostructure gives to the union, it can also give without a union or to avoid having a union."[7]

Secondly, the development of professional or bureaucratic rather than entrepreneurial management leads to a firm loyalty adverse to unionization. The loyalty to a firm replaces the loyalty to the occupation. "Among machinists, toolmakers, steam fitters and other skilled workers there was the sense of common interest arising from a shared skill. As machinery replaces both repetitive and drudging work and eliminates skilled occupations, it lowers these barriers to identification."[8]

Thirdly, Galbraith argues, the growth of white-collar, professional, technical and engineering workers characteristic of the technostructure represents "a massive shift from workers who are within the reach of unions to those who are not."[9] This results from the identification of the white-collar worker with the technostructure which, in turn, masks the line between management and workers.

Fourthly, Galbraith maintains that the individual need for union support has been reduced by the comparative affluence and relatively steady employment that is derived from the industrial state and the regulation of aggregate demand. Not only does the worker not need the "shared privation" of strike pay or the soup kitchen, but also, by permitting employment changes with relative ease, the "high employment and high income are solvents for the sense of compulsion and thus are substitutes for the union."[10]

It is perhaps interesting to note that the major economic downturn in the United States in 1974 and 1975 which accompanied the winding down and ending of American involvement in southeast Asia and which was precipitated by the inflationary impact of the energy crisis, has led to new demands from American labour for increased stabilization activity by the government, such as the massive tax reduction bill. In short, labour wants more Keynesianism, not less. Should this fail, however, faith in the system may also fade.

Finally, Galbraith suggests that through advertising and salesmanship, the demand of workers as consumers is kept at a level equal to or, preferably, in excess of current income. The result is the growth of consumer debt which helps ensure reliable and materialistic workers willing to be bought off.[11]

In total, Galbraith concludes that the new industrial state is hostile to the continued existence of a significant labour movement.

The industrial system, it seems clear, is unfavourable to the union. Power passes to the technostructure and thus lessens the conflict of interest between employer and employee which gives the union much of its reason for existence. Capital and technology allows the firm to substitute white-collar workers and machines that cannot be organized for blue-collar workers that can. The regulation of aggregate demand, the resulting high level of employment together with the general increase in well-being all, on balance, make the union less necessary or less powerful or both.[12]

[Furthermore], production workers in areas of advanced technology—computer and data processing industries, instrumentation, telementry, specified electronics and the like—are not easily organized.[13]

One significant qualification that appears more as an afterthought than a major reservation must be mentioned: "not all unions are within the industrial system and those outside have a better prospect."[14]

It is clear that the modern corporation does represent a threat to the existing union structure, in the same sense that the emergence of the mass production industries between the wars threatened the existing craft structure. But that is not to say that the technical and organizational changes that have taken place have not opened up a whole range of new opportunities for new union forms; indeed, there is every indication that such new forms are emerging in Canada although not necessarily as part of the established union structure.[15] Before examining the prospect of white-collar unions, however, let us dispose of some of the reasons suggested by Galbraith for the decline of organized labour.

The argument that the separation of ownership from management of the large corporations has diminished the conflict of interest between labour and management, permitting management to pay generously without a union so as to maintain uninterrupted labour services, is not very convincing. With few exceptions, labour costs remain a significant cost factor and when demand fluctuates, labour is the first to suffer through cutbacks. In any case, as Professor John Porter has demonstrated, the link between Canada's economic elite and the corporate boardrooms is extremely strong.[16]

Nor is this the only area of conflict between labour and management. Technological change, which is central to the new technology, has created a major point of difference that cuts across occupational lines. Computer technology, for example, is as destructive of white-collar skills as mechanization has been of blue-collar skills. Professor Leo Johnson makes this point strongly: "the process of proletarianization-through-automation that destroyed the craft workers in the nineteenth century may be repeated among the white collar workers in the twentieth."[17] And as anyone who is familiar with labour history and contemporary disputes is aware, technological displacement has been of central importance to the creation, growth and militance of labour organizations. Also, while management *can* give benefits to employees without a union, it is not clear that it will continue to do so at a time, or of a size, sufficient to maintain differentials with other workers, unionized or not. Failure to do so has been a significant factor in the emergence of a number of new unions and quasi-unions, particularly among middle management and engineering staffs.

It may be difficult to separate the effect of narrowing wage differentials for such groups from the effect of the growth of bureaucracy. As corporations increase in size there develops a need for more complex communication and coordination mechanisms. As a result the higher employee loses his uniqueness and becomes one link in a chain of decision-making. David Solomon, in writing about professional employees, has argued that

Our social life is to an increasing extent dominated by bureaucratic institutions. . . . By definition, professional and bureaucracies are incompatible. . . . Consequently there is likely to be an uneasy tension between managerial authorities and professional identity; but whether he [the professional] does or not, he threatens to usurp some of the power of those who invited him into the house in the first place.[18]

This argument has been made by numerous observers. It is also difficult to see how grievances arising from large corporate (or government) bureaucracies can be settled unilaterally within these same bureaucracies. At the same time we might note that grievance procedure has often been called the bread and butter of North American unionism. Nor can we ignore the effects of alienation and routinization that are a by-product of large-scale enterprise on white-collar, professional, technical or blue-collar workers in their search for meaningful identification with their jobs. The alternative remains the union or related forms of employee organization.

The problem of alienation leads us to a major diversion at this point. As early as the turn of the century, Veblen was aware of the tendency for the machine process (as he called it) to subdivide, routinize and standardize work. Despite all the problems in subjecting labour to the needs of the machine process, "it is bargained for, delivered, and turned to account on schedules of time, speed, and intensity which are continually sought to be reduced to a more precise measurement and a more sweeping uniformity."[19] It is safe to say now that it is not only the production process but equally the administrative process that has been rendered precise, compartmentalized, and of alienating uniformity. The decline in the meaningfulness of the routinized task and the breakdown of personal contact between employer and employee have served to dull, if not destroy entirely, the ethic of craft workmanship and the sense of importance, of contribution. As one Canadian unionist notes,

we are producing things that are not useful: we get no particular thrill out of producing them. We're producing them because we need a job. If we're making cars, we'd rather make good cars than some garbage that's going to fall apart on the highway in three years. If we're delivering mail, we'd like to deliver the mail properly so it gets to people easily. If we work in the university, we want to work so the university becomes a place where people learn things. All people—not just kids who come from rich homes. And not the type of learning that pumps kids full of management or government propaganda, so they can be sent out to become managers. Now that's the way we all feel and yet there's no account of this in industry.[20]

The result has been rising absenteeism, alcoholism, drug addiction and sabotage. And there has been shown a direct relationship between deteriorating mental health and closely supervised and routinized jobs.[21]

The primitive responses listed above to work alienation are entirely personal and since they occur probably as frequently among unionized as non-unionized employees, reflect the unions' unwillingness or inability to deal with work alienation. Today's dominant labour organizations emerged in the pre-affluent society period, before workers had much more than the necessities of life. But by now, many organized workers have considerable discretionary income. Hence,

... in the opulent or affluent society real scarcity has been succeeded by contrived scarcity and the successful functioning of our economy depends on reiterating the contrivance. Increasing income implies the gratification of ever less and less essential wants. . . . The decision-taking structures become even more bureaucratic. Labour itself becomes a produced means of production, an item of human capital equipment.[22]

Union organization which emerged in a period of scarcity finds it difficult to adapt its attitudes and operations to a period of relative affluence.[23] Gone is the immediacy of the bread box and hence workers are demanding both more leisure, without any reduction in real income, and a qualitative improvement in the work environment. They now bargain for such things as job variation and rotation, control over hiring and firing, the rate of technical change, discipline and even product quality and price. This poses a real conflict between the crude efficiency-minded technostructure programmed to implement the input-minimizing process and to consider labour as a completely variable and malleable factor—and the worker seeking to exchange potential increases in real material income for more human but less efficient working conditions. Because trade unions are well integrated into the industrial relations system which is dedicated to preventing as much overt conflict as possible, they consequently tend to restrict the role of unions to the role they had won by the end of the Second World War when the present system was institutionalized. Management is vehemently opposed to extending the scope of bargaining to include the areas of current concern—control of the conditions and security of the job—because these are the critical decisions for the success of the multinational corporation. Labour unions fought and in part won the battle against the entrepreneurial employer who varied his workers' wages as a means of competitive strategy. But even as they won it this lever had ceased to become important; it coincided with the ascendency of the multinational corporation, which can vary wages and sundry other costs through plant shutdowns, layoffs, transfers of operations and international mobility of capital to lower wage areas. As an Ontario labour study reported for the electronics industry, the recent employment decline "can partly be attributed to a change in technology, but is largely due to substitution of foreign imports. What is ironic is that *the imports are from foreign manufacturers which have corporate connections with the parent companies of Canada's plants that are affected.*[24]

So far the Canadian labour movement has been unable to develop a viable approach or even an understanding of the need for worker control. It is probably this, as much as any other factor, that has hindered the Canadian Labour Congress's attempt to organize white-collar workers, the group that has in the past always had significantly more control over its working conditions and considerably more security from unemployment

down of loyalty to the firm and loyalty to the worker group or union. It is precisely the destruction of skills and the transformation of work patterns that have had such profound effect in the initiation and radicalization of labour organization, from the famous Luddite uprisings to the recent strikes by the CNR railway workers in protest against the railway run-throughs. In contrast, there is every indication that modern technology is increasing the amount of drudging and repetitive work and destroying white-collar skills. Stenographers, filing clerks, air controllers, waitresses, sales clerks and office cleaners all face repetitive and unrewarding routine tasks. Further, the challenge to firm loyalty that results from the growth of large-scale business enterprise and the resulting bureaucracy is attested to by the traditional argument that the biggest barrier to unionism is small size and loyalty to the entrepreneur of the small firm. Size tends to destroy this identification.

In summary, on *a priori* grounds there are few reasons to suspect that white-collar workers will not organize. First, dangerous, dirty or unpleasant working conditions are unlikely to be a factor as they have been in mining, longshoring or some construction occupations. But, in the past, white-collar workers have generally been better paid (relatively), had greater job security, shorter hours and, probably, greater fringe benefits. Also of importance was the greater opportunity for advancement through promotion. These advantages have been eroded by two forces: the growth of the white-collar stratum of industry, and the enormous increase in the supply of such a stratum, at the public's expense, through the public education system. A plumber requires four years apprenticeship; a stenographer can learn virtually all her skills in secondary school. The net effect of this and of the activity of blue-collar unionism has been a narrowing and even a reversal of the differential advantages.

Secondly, the growth in size of the white-collar sector has resulted in more factory-like conditions, the standardization of work rules, division of labour, hierarchy of authority and the physical and structural grouping of employees. Thirdly, the growth has resulted in white-collar labour costs rising to a point where they can no longer be ignored by employers. White-collar employees, too, become subject to employment fluctuations as do blue-collar workers, although this is less evident because white-collar workers are concentrated in those industries where employment fluctuations are traditionally moderate because of the nature of the demand. Finally, the opportunity for promotional advancement, while still more open to white-collar workers, has definitely declined. The employment pyramid no longer has the narrow base. For technological reasons the base has widened, perceptively diminishing the potential opportunity for any given employee. As the perception of opportunity declines, the perceived benefits from unionism may be expected to increase. As one observer has noted, "the more general point is that the elements which have traditionally insulated white-collar workers from problems generating a collective response are losing much of their force."[26] A study of engineers and professions yielded a similar conclusion.[27]

Empirical results also support this conclusion. In the Scandinavian countries, especially Sweden, white-collar workers have proved more amenable to organization than blue-collar workers have in Canada. Certainly, government office workers have proved easy to unionize in Canada as have school teachers. The above suggests that the pessimism with which Galbraith and others view the future of this kind of unionism reflects a combination of a restrictive ideological, social and legal climate in the United States towards labour, and a failure in the prevailing union institutions to adjust to the needs of this kind of worker.

Nevertheless, even in the United States white-collar workers have organized. Professor Barbash has concluded that they have been most readily organized when they have: (a) a distinctive professional, technical or artistic identification; (b) a close proximity to unionized manual workers; and (c) a high concentration of workers in close physical association.[28] Contrary to Galbraith's expectations, these conditions have been most often achieved within the larger corporation. Moreover, the growth of white-collar groups with the development of the technostructure may be expected to accentuate these favourable influences rather than diminish them.

Gus Tyler, long-time American labour activist, has made similar observations:

First, workers in the service trades and in the professions have been and are organizing into unions, most of them affiliated with the AFL-CIO. In other words, many of the workers in the new labour force are moving or have already moved into the mainstream of labour.

Second, professional workers have been organizing into associations that act like unions even though they disclaim union identity. They bargain, they strike, they sign contracts. They are unions in everything but name.

Third, the nature of work in service and the professions makes these workers highly susceptible to the union idea. These new ones may indeed turn out to be the most numerous, the most articulate, and the most political-minded sector of the American labour movement.[29]

There are two other arguments relating to the future of North American unionism within the new industrial state; first, that the regulation of aggregate and specific demand and the proliferation of advertising have produced a secure, docile and willing labour force, reducing the demand for labour unions; and second, that the growth of the modern corporation has brought the majority of workers within its fold.

The attempted regulation of demand to reduce employment fluctuations has until recently been accompanied by moderate but steady increases in prices.[30] Studies show a close relationship between price increases and union growth since price increases have the effect of reducing the economic welfare of all workers, regardless of type. As Davis has reported, "the evidence seems to indicate that changes in union membership correlate more closely with sharp changes in prices than with 'prosperity'. . . . Rising prices correlate more closely with union growth than does the prosperity phase of the business cycle partly because prices affect all workers, while the cycle is much more violent in some industries than in others."[31] In any case, over the last decade Canadian experience in reducing unemployment insecurity through the regulation of aggregate demand has been notoriously bad. Further, the recent acceleration of inflation has the effect of increasing the demand for unionism as a protective device.

Similarly, the effect of the regulation of specific demand (for a product) through advertising, which Galbraith has deemed indispensible to the heavily capitalized modern corporation, can be expected to increase the demand for unionism rather than reduce it. Demand-creating or shifting advertising comes predominantly from the multinationals and depicts a level of consumption well above that made possible by the average income— high performance cars, prepared foods, luxury or credit services, travel, cosmetics, furs, et cetera. While this "demonstration effect" might well induce the average worker to work harder to achieve the desired consumption levels, it also has the unsettling affect of encouraging workers to demand larger and larger incomes in order to achieve this level. In the face of this kind of advertising, workers tend to become *psychologically* less well off. To become aggressive and achieve the pictured norm, it is necessary to organize to press for higher incomes.

The pervasiveness of the modern corporation should not blind us to the fact that, because the modern corporation is capital intensive, its contribution to employment is considerably less important than its contribution to output. Thus, the technostructure that Galbraith emphasizes is restricted to the oligopolistic industrial system: "nearly all communications, production and distribution of electric power, much transportation, most manufacturing and mining, a substantial share of retail trade and a considerable amount of entertainment are conducted or provided by large firms."[32]

Professor Rosenbluth, in his study of concentration in Canadian industries, provides a quantification of the industrial state areas of the Canadian economy which, while similar to Galbraith's, has a few differences.[33] These, however, are not likely to make any significant difference in overall results. Although Rosenbluth's data are quite old there is little reason to believe that any major shift has taken place in the structure of particular industries that would seriously bias the following estimates. By industry, Rosenbluth concludes that: in retail trade, 80 per cent of business is conducted under independent control; in wholesale trade, "by far the greater part of the business is done by small firms"; in the service industries, excluding government, two-thirds are in areas "where there is clearly no question of large firms or high concentration," while three-quarters of the remaining services are done by small firms; in transportation and communication, some sectors such as trucking are clearly not concentrated ("103 large carriers account for only 68 per cent of the total gross revenue"), while others such as railways and airlines are of fairly high concentration but many are publicly owned.[34]

Other industries, except agriculture, fishing and trapping, and construction, can be considered within the industrial concentrated sector. "Making a rough and ready breakdown, we can say that about three-fifths of Canada's output (except government administration and defence) originates in sectors dominated by large corporations . . . while two-fifths originates in sectors in which small firms predominate."[35] Since 1951, when the statistics were collected for Rosenbluth's study, the tertiary sector, including service and government, has increased in relative importance, in employment if not in output. The majority of all new job creation in recent years has been in the tertiary sector.

On the basis of the 1961 census and using Rosenbluth's categories, the following results can be obtained for the labour force distribution.

Table 1

(000's)

	(1) Labour Force	(2) Wage & Salary Earners	(3) White-Collar in (2)	(4) (3) minus Managerial and Professional	(5) Blue-Collar in (2)	(6) "Organizable" =(4)+(5)
Concentrated Sector	2,467	2,260	856	580	1,366	1,946
Non-Concentrated Sector (Excl. Agric.)	2,722	2,260	1,567	1,056	668	1,724
Government	483	483	368	292	110	402
Total (incl. Agric.)*	6,472	5,367	2,788	1,938	2,421	4,359

*Unclassified occupations and industries excluded

SOURCE: *Census of Canada*, 1961.

What is significant is that employment in the non-technostruc-
ture industries is equally as important as that which fits within
the definition of the new industrial state. Secondly, blue-collar
workers remain almost twice as important within the concentrated industries as white-collar employment, particularly if we
exclude from white-collar employees the managerial and professional group. Thirdly, there are twice the number of theo-
retically organizable white-collar workers in the non-concen-
trated sector as there are in the concentrated sector. Finally, the
government sector (9 per cent of wage and salary earners in 1961
and growing) has been amenable to organization whether white-
or blue-collar. The industrial state is not then the pervasive
influence in terms of employment, and even less so when we consider the areas of potential organization. It is readily apparent
from a comparison of Tables 1 and 2 that the greatest scope
for union organization lies outside the large multinational
corporations.

Table 2

	Union Membership, 1970 (000's)
Concentrated Sector	811
Transportation and Utilities*	363
Non-Concentrated Sector (excl. Agric.)	552
Government	322
Total (including unreported)	2,173

*Includes some industries (e.g., trucking) of low concentration, estimated
as less than 25 per cent of union membership in this classification.

SOURCE: *Labour Gazette*, April 1971.

The conclusion we come to, therefore, is that the new industrial state *per se* does not pose the threat to the existence of
unions that Galbraith forecast. Indeed, the growing proletarian-
ization of white-collar occupations because of the growth of
bureaucracy which is, after all, the white-collar equivalent to
the compartmentalization and fragmentation of blue-collar
employment as a result of production line techniques, has obviously widened the potential for unionization. Within this
general system, however, we must explore the effects of tech-

nological homogenization upon the branch plant economy—that is, on Canada and the Canadian union structure.

Professor Levitt, in applying the logic of the dynamics of the large corporation to the Canadian market, has shown the corporate need for multinational expansion—the need to spawn subsidiaries both to provide a steady flow of material inputs and to guarantee a market for capital and intermediate products. The modern corporation requires stability of market share and diversification by geographical region and product. But in consequence, "the risk is not so much eliminated, as shifted to small-scale entrepreneurs and to the peripheral or hinterland economies."[36] But at the same time, "the executives of branch plants are managers, not entrepreneurs. . . . They do not formulate policy, they administer it. The decisions they make are routine in the sense that they are constrained by budgetary allocation made at head office."[37] The fact that decision-making is in large part restricted to the metropolis erodes the scope and freedom of policy choice in the branch-plant economy. These factors have provided the setting for the operation of the Canadian system of industrial relations in the post-Second World War period.[38]

CANADIAN LABOUR AND INTERNATIONAL UNIONISM

The pervasive influence of American labour institutions in Canada is almost as old as the Canadian labour movement itself. It dates from the mid-nineteenth century when a combination of factors—the mobility of workers across a scarcely visible international boundary, the integration of economies during the period of partial continental free trade and the wide dispersal and weakness of indigenous Canadian labour organizations—prompted the establishment of fraternal integration, particularly among the skilled trades. Already by the 1880s, under the tariff-supported growth of Canadian industry, the Canadian subsidiary of the American corporation had begun to appear in significant numbers. Across Canada the union movement began to evolve as a Canadian compromise, exhibiting much in common with the American Federation of Labor (AFL) craft unions but also co-existing with purely Canadian unions or with Canadian assemblies of the nineteenth-century labour organization, the Knights of Labor. This compromise ended with what Idele Wilson has called the first crisis of Canadian labour in 1902 when the Trades and Labor Congress of Canada bowed to AFL demands to expel all "dual" unions: that is, unions not affiliated with the AFL but with overlapping jurisdiction.[39] Seventy years of recurring friction have followed this decision.

In 1919 the second major crisis developed with the revolt of western labour in the breakaway One Big Union (OBU), an industrial union movement, in response to the failure of the craft-oriented American business unionism to solve the instability problems of the western hinterland.[40] The defeat of of the western secessionist movement temporarily dampened dissent until the nationalist faction in the All Canadian Congress of Labour (ACCL) allied itself to the breakaway industrial unions of the Congress of Industrial Organizations (CIO) to form the Canadian Congress of Labour (CCL).[41] It is important to note that the "invasion" by CIO unions in the 1930s was simply a response "to pressing invitations sent by Canadian workers who had more confidence in the capabilities and strength of American unions than they had in their own. . . . Whenever American unions moved into Canada, Canadians themselves usually did the organizing and paid the bill out of their own pockets."[42]

The industrial unionism of the CIO, while international, was compatible with the interests of unorganized workers in the primary industries of the west and the mass-production industries of eastern Canada. In a very real sense, the spread of CIO unions in Canada marks the coming to maturity of the multinational companies in this country. The mature corporations in the United States, under pressure from the Keynesian liberals, began reluctantly to accept industrial unions as a necessary concomitant of the regulation of aggregate demand.[43] The Canadian branch plants followed.

The CIO was organized in the United States because of the failure of the autarchic, exclusive and obsolete craft union structure to organize the mass-production worker or to deal with the problems facing the primary-industry worker, organized or unorganized. As a result, the CIO adopted industrial unionism, a more political stance, and a more democratic structure with considerably more local autonomy, particularly for Canadian districts which, given the CIO's problems in the United States, the parent unions were not too concerned with anyway. Thus, within the CIO structure, Canada's unorganized production workers could find a suitable industrial organization and her primary-industry workers could find a union movement willing to fight for welfare statism to cushion against the instability of their industries. The autonomy was possible because, despite the already considerable degree of American control of the Canadian economy, the multinational corporation had not yet evolved to the present degree of global integration, nor had the economies become so integrated that independent policy had become (or was perceived to have become) impossible. It is only since the late 1950s that the web of interconnections, corporate and government, has become so dominant.

With the rapid advance in computer and communications technology the web has been strengthened. Increased efficiency of worldwide bureaucratic control and supervision systems has permitted further global integration. As Levitt has documented, this process of integration has proceeded to the point of "recolonization" of Canada within America's new mercantilism.

The satellitic status of Canada is reinforced, as in the old mercantile system, by the network of exclusivist favours, preferences and privileges negotiated from a position of weakness *vis-à-vis* the United States. The vulnerability of Canada to changes in American tariffs, quotas, credit conditions, defense orders and capital movements increases as commercial exports by Canadian-controlled enterprise are replaced by inter-company transfer and politically negotiated barter deals.[44]

As long as the postwar and Korean booms continued, exports remained easy and heavy capital inflows persisted, there was no significant conflict of interest between Canadian workers and their international unions. The problems began to arise when the American economy ran up against the limits of imperial expansion, as Europe and Japan recovered—limits partly obscured by the buoyancy of Vietnam military expenditure during the 1960s.

It is in the period after 1965, after the United States began issuing guidelines to its multinational corporations, that the scope of Canadian economic policy becomes increasingly smaller. Thus, although uneasiness as to the long-run implications of American foreign and economic policy was repeatedly expressed in union conventions and even occasionally by labour spokesmen in official statements, criticism was not directed at the international unions or at the economic integration but at the American, and less frequently, at the Canadian governments. The dominant labour position was that because workers in both countries were dealing with the same company, often producing the same product, or at least sharing the massive resources of a conglomerate corporation, the workers were best united in one union, matching the corporate structure. Indeed, there is a greater tendency to have Canadian national unions in those industries least dominated by multinational corporations.

The American dollar crisis and unemployment problems of the early 1970s which produced a protectionist reaction, have raised completely new challenges to the international labour connection. The dominant American sections of the international unions have vigorously, and financially, supported a series of protective measures: the tariff surcharge introduced by President Nixon in 1971 as a short-run measure, followed by the DISC (Domestic International Sales Corporations) program, (the purpose of which being to shift production from subsidiary plants in foreign countries to U.S. plants through a program of tax incentives), and the revision of the Auto Pact to increase the American employment component. Most recently has been the AFL-CIO support for the Burke-Hartke Bill which would penalize the multinational corporations, described by the AFL-CIO as "modern day dinosaurs which eat the jobs of American workers."[45] Yet the foreign country with the greatest concentration of the multinationals is Canada. In short, the AFL-CIO members are out after Canadian jobs, most of which are filled by their own members. In a recent study prepared for the Ontario Federation of Labour on plant shutdowns in Ontario, June 1970 to June 1971, 55 per cent of the plants and 63 per cent of the workers affected were employed by American multinational corporations. Sixty-seven per cent of the plants were unionized—overwhelmingly by international unions.[46] Thus we have the fascinating spectacle of Canadian union members remitting their monthly membership dues to help finance a campaign to abolish their jobs. Canadian workers as a whole, therefore, find themselves in much the same position as did the western workers before 1919, or the resource and mass-production workers in the 1930s, in an economic hinterland of the new industrial state centred in the United States. The stability of the new mercantilism, as with the old, does not extend to the periphery. Thus we see the emergence of a new breakaway movement among the trade unions: the pulp and paper workers, various types of metal workers, retail-wholesale trade workers and, most recently, the aluminum workers in Kitimat.[47] If this analysis is correct, we can expect to see a fourth crisis in Canadian labour as the Canadian union movement seeks to defend itself once more against the instability of employment and earnings characteristic of the hinterland.

NOTES

1. At least four multinational companies, General Motors, American Telephone and Telegraph, Standard Oil and Ford Motors, have budgets that exceed that of the Canadian government.
2. Daniel Bell, Introduction to the Harbinger edition of Thorstein Veblen, *The Engineers and the Price System* (New York: Harcourt, Brace, 1963), p. 34.
3. Thorstein Veblen's major contributions occur in *The Theory of Business Enterprise* (1904), *Absentee Ownership* (1923), and *The Engineers and the Price System* (1921). Berle and Means' book, *The Modern Corporation and Private Property* was published in 1934. Joseph Schumpeter is best known for his *The Theory of Economic Development* (1934) and *Capitalism, Socialism and Democracy* (1942).
4. J. K. Galbraith, *The New Industrial State* (New York: Signet, 1968). Other books by Galbraith of interest are *The Affluent Society* (1958) and *American Capitalism* (1952). The term labour, of course, is ambiguous, meaning variously that abstract factor, labour power, that is neither land nor capital; that part of the labour force that works for others directly (or what in Europe is called the working class); or that part of the work force which belongs to union organizations. The first meaning is of purely theoretical interest. Rather it is the structure and

distribution of the working class and of labour unions, and of the inter-action between the two that concern us here.

5. Galbraith, *The New Industrial State*, p. 21.

6. It is interesting to note that businesses in the United States look quite favourably upon the price and wage controls initiated by Nixon in 1971, despite the fact that such controls might traditionally be con-sidered anathema in a free enterprise economy. In fact, corporate leaders seemed content with the relative stability in prices, wage costs and demand that the controls were designed to provide—at least so long as profit margins were not squeezed significantly.

7. Galbraith, *New Industrial State*, p. 275.

8. Ibid.

9. Ibid., p. 276.

10. Ibid., p. 278.

11. Ibid., p. 281.

12. Ibid., p. 283.

13. Ibid., p. 285.

14. Ibid., p. 284.

15. "The Department of Labour is aware, however, that a number of organizations concerned with occupational or professional standards now engage in some form of collective bargaining, negotiation or con-sultation on wages and conditions of employment. The question of their inclusion or exclusion in subsequent [*Labour Organization*] reports is under consideration." *Labour Organization in Canada*, 1971, p. xii.

16. John Porter, *The Vertical Mosaic* (Toronto: University of Toronto Press, 1965), p. 255. Even where labour costs are not that significant, corporations resist paying labour more than the minimum required, except where premiums may be paid to prevent a union from being organized within the firm. A few years ago in the oil distilling industry in Canada, the mediator of a wage dispute between the oil workers' union and the company involved was told by the employer that although it could easily pay the union wage demand, it was prepared to suffer a strike because it didn't think that production workers should be paid such high wages. The difference was a few cents an hour between the union demand and the company offer.

17. Leo Johnson, "The Development of Class in Canada in the Twentieth Century," *People's Canada* (Aug. 1-12), 1972.

18. David Solomon, quoted in Gus Tyler, *The Labor Revolution* (New York: Viking Press, 1966), p. 173.

19. Thorstein Veblen, *The Theory of Business Enterprise* (New York: Mentor, 1958), pp. 11-12.

20. André Beckerman, "An Organizer's Guide to Workers' Control," *Canadian Dimension*, vol. 8, No. 7 (June 1972), p. 19.

21. John Case, "Workers Control: Toward a North American Movement," *Our Generation*, vol. 8, No. 3 (1972), p. 4.

22. Kari Levitt, *Silent Surrender* (Toronto: Macmillan, 1970), p. 30.

23. Trade union members, at least within the skilled crafts and the large corporations, tend to have higher wages than their unorganized brothers. Whether this is a result of union power or a result of the market power of the oligopolistic firm is a debatable point. See H. M. Levinson, "Unionism Concentration and Wage Changes: Towards a Unified Theory," *Industrial and Labour Relations Review*, Jan. 1967.

24. John Eleen and Ashley Bernadine, *Shutdown* (Ontario Federation of Labour, 1971), p. 21 (Emphasis added.)

25. Johnson, "Class in Canada," pp. 7*ff*.

26. A. Kleingartner, "The Organization of White Collar Workers," B. C. Roberts, ed., *Industrial Relations: Contemporary Issues* (New York: St. Martin's, 1968), p. 157.

27. E. M. Kassalow, "Perspective on the Upsurge of Public Employee Unionism," in R. T. Woodward and R. B. Peterson, eds., *Collective Negotiation for Public and Professional Employees* (Glenview: Scott, Foresman and Co., 1969), p. 24. In commenting on the failure to organize engineers he writes: "The occupations continue to enjoy a generally more favourable labor market than some of the other professionals and this may account for their relative quiet."

28. See summary in Kleingartner, "Organization of White Collar Workers," p. 158.

29. Tyler, *The Labor Revolution,* p. 158.

30. It can be, and indeed has been, argued that any attempt to regulate demand and unemployment in a changing economy through Keynesian policies must produce a steady rise in the price level, but as long as this inflation is kept within reasonable limits and does not vary widely, it poses no threat to the modern corporation. Persistent inflation of the kind experienced in 1974 and to the present (May 1975), however, does create much more serious problems.

31. H. B. Davis, "The Theory of Union Growth," QJE, August 1941, pp. 7-8.

32. Galbraith, *New Industrial State*, p. 21.

33. Gideon Rosenbluth, "Concentration and Monopoly in the Canadian Economy," in M. Oliver, ed., *Social Purpose for Canada*, (Toronto: University of Toronto Press, 1961).

34. Ibid., pp. 243-48.

35. Ibid., p. 203.

36. Levitt, *Silent Surrender,* p. 72.

37. Ibid., p. 77.

38. For the most part, we will be considering the labour movement in English Canada only. Since the early 1960s, the emergence of a French-Canadian nationalist alternative to international unionism and its subsequent politicization distinguishes it from the rest of organized labour in Canada. Indeed, it may be a harbinger of things to come in English Canada.

39. Idele Wilson, "Labour Organization in Canada," *Annals of the American Academy of Political and Social Science,* September 1947, p. 99.

40. See my "National Policy and the Development of the Western Canadian Labour Movement," Western Canadian Studies Conference, Calgary, 1970.

41. The tension between the nationalists and the industrial unionists of the CIO is described in I. Abella, "Lament for a Union Movement," in I. Lumsden, ed., *Close the 49th Parallel, etc.* (Toronto: University of Toronto Press, 1970).

42. I. Abella, "CIO Reluctant Invaders," *Canadian Dimension,* March-April, 1972, p. 20.

43. Galbraith, *New Industrial State,* pp. 308 ff.

44. Levitt, *Silent Surrender,* pp. 38-9.

45. *Winnipeg Tribune,* December 5, 1972.

46. Eleen and Bernadine, *Shutdown,* pp. 3-4.

47. So far, the major breakaways have taken place in the resource industries geographically removed from the centre of union administration. This probably reflects both the inferior servicing these unions had been receiving from the internationals and the greater difficulty the central offices had in closely monitoring the attitudes of the local membership.

Edouard Cloutier

Industrialization, Technology and Contemporary French-Canadian Nationalism

Industrialization has settled one question once and for all: Quebec is part of Canada, however uneasy the bonds may lie. Nobody ever mentions now the dreams of twenty years ago, the Republic of Laurentia. What nationalist Quebec talks of now is a Republic of Canada.

Miriam Chapin, Quebec Now, p. 178.

It is the intent of this essay to provide a general introduction to the relationship between industrialization, technology and contemporary French-Canadian nationalism, and to briefly analyse how the program of the Parti-Québécois proposes a solution to many of the human problems of an industrial and technological society through a policy of independence for Quebec. The first part of the essay examines much of the major work of the past decade which has sought to explain the relationship between industrialism and French-Canadian nationalism and establishes a typology of the different explanations offered. In light of these explanations, the second part then goes on to present and analyse those parts of the Parti Québécois program dealing with the problems of industrialism and technology.

INDUSTRIALISM AS AN EXPLANATION OF THE CHANGES IN FRENCH-CANADIAN NATIONALISM

Miriam Chapin, in conclusion to a sweeping analysis of the contemporary social situation in Quebec, wrote the above lines in 1956. Before the Quiet Revolution, such judgment seems to have been accepted by most observers of the Quebec scene, be they outsiders or insiders, English-speaking or French-speaking. They expected that industrialization would produce shifts in occupational emphasis and a broader educational system which would in turn lead French Canadians to assimilate North American language and culture. George Kelly recalls English Canadians' "first glance thesis" which held that "urbanization would bring the quiet sleep of surviving provincialism and gentle Americanization."[1]

For some analysts of the early and mid-sixties, even the advent of the Quiet Revolution does not seem to have altered this outlook. The historian James Corry, for example, believed that "if Quebec has managed to keep its culture so far, it is because of its agrarian society. But now [in 1961], Quebec is caught in the logic of interdependent economic and large scale industrial enterprises"[2] For sociologist John Porter, it seemed evident at the time that ". . . as Quebec becomes more industrialized, it will become culturally more like other industrial societies. At that time, similarities in social characteristics which its urbanized population will share with the other provinces may be far more important in terms of social development than whatever differences remain."[3] Similar views were shared by Gerald Clark and Peter Russell, both of whom predicted a decline in French-Canadian nationalism due to modernization. Closely related to such reasoning is the belief that economic progress would temper French-Canadian nationalism. For example, Norman Smith noted that the reaction of some English Canadians to the *Preliminary Report of the Royal Commission on Bilingualism and Biculturalism* was that "things could not be that bad with the coming of economic progress" that all of Canada enjoyed at the time.[4] Likewise, Peter Desbarats was astounded at the discovery that English Quebeckers did not seem to understand that the economic development of Quebec in the early sixties would "kill the Anglostocracy."

It seems, however, that the majority of analysts at that time had reversed the earlier accepted idea that increasing industrialization would lead to a decline of French-Canadian nationalism; they did not think that industrialization, urbanization,

modernization or the economic prosperity which is supposed
to go hand-in-hand with these socio-economic phenomena
would contribute to a lowering of the French-Canadian sense
of nationality. Gerald Craig noticed that these factors had not
resulted in the assimilation of French Canadians up until then
and Eric Kierans predicted that they did not imply the death
of French-Canadian culture either. On the contrary, George
Kelly, Abraham Rotstein and E. M. Corbett found that the
growth of French-Canadian nationalism parallelled that of
industrialization. Prime Minister Pearson went even further by
arguing that English-Canadian behavior based on "matter-of-
fact assimilation of French Canadians into industrial North
America breeds separatism."[5]

Even though such ideas are commonplace today, it is important to note that it was not always so; the turnabout began to
occur around 1963, that is, about three years after the coming to
power of the Lesage government (June 1960) and four years
after the death of Duplessis (September 1959)—two dates which
are generally recognized as the start of the Quiet Revolution, a
period characterized by substantial economic, social, ideological,
religious and cultural changes within Quebec. Up until the first
terrorist acts of March 8, 1963, according to Hugh Myers, English Canadians considered the Quiet Revolution as they would
"the dangers of fallout and cigarette smoking." It appears clear,
therefore, that the development of a new period in the social
history of Quebec has produced significant changes within
Quebec.

There have been many different attempts to reassess the relationship between industrialization and French-Canadian
nationalism. The following are but ten of those attempts, and
while they do not encompass all of the rethinking, they at least
illustrate the nature and the range of contemporary thought
about French-Canadian nationalism and how it is affected by
industrial and technological change.

1. Nationalism as a survival reaction to industrialism

Some analysts (for example, Eric Kierans and E. M. Corbett)
have attributed the coextensive increase in the two factors to
the French-Canadian permanent struggle to survive. They pre-

sent French Canada as fearing for its cultural life and identity in the face of mounting economic and social changes engendered by the ever-expanding implantation of industrialization and technology. Fear would engender aggressive attitudes, hence French-Canadian nationalism.

2. Nationalism as the ultimate, but doomed, anti-industrial stand

While a cultural survival reaction to industrialism can produce a form of nationalism which endures long enough to permit the erection of a vast array of defence mechanisms, it can also engender, whenever the danger is perceived as overpowering, a final, extremely violent and determined, do-or-die stand. Such an analysis is made in the November 1963 editorial of *The Mountie*, the official organ of the RCMP, which views the Quiet Revolution—and, more precisely, separatism—as French Canada's last desperate kick before a slow but sure death under the steamroller of the North American industrial way of life.[6] This view differs from Chapin's only in as much as it allows for an ephemeral surge of nationalism as a proof of its imminent disappearance.

3. Nationalism based on industrialization as a means of salvation

A third outlook introduces the possibility of a reversal of attitude toward industrialization on the part of French Canada. In its first stage, industrialization was considered as culturally alien and therefore assimilatory and dangerous. The corresponding attitude was one of outright rejection at worst or negative submission at best. Then, as industrialization enters a more advanced phase—let us qualify it as technological—it becomes a means of salvation whereby the culture can escape the industrial pressure or even integrate it in a positive fashion. This curious turnabout occurs when progress pushes beyond the mere mechanization of the means of production and toward the reorganization of the involvement of people in the production process. At this stage, the accent is transferred from the quantity of machines to the quality of their operators and organizers. Groups which once felt financially incapable of acquiring the complex machinery of mechanical production tend to view the techno-logical phase of industrialization as possibly liberating.[7] This belief arises because they now feel that through an adequate system of education they can produce sufficient technocrats to operate the industrial system and greatly expand production for their own purposes.

4. Nationalism as the product of the industrial social revolution

In the fourth approach, the link between French-Canadian nationalism and industrialism is explained through the "social revolution" which French Canada underwent during the Quiet Revolution. In a general way, according to Kenneth McRae, "ideologically, French Canada has not yet come to terms with the new industrial society."[8] The advent of this new type of society has badly damaged the cultural tissue of the group, thus causing extensive social disequilibrium erupting into national-ism. According to Abraham Rotstein, technological change has somersaulted French Canada from a pre-liberal to a post-liberal outlook in too short a time to permit smooth social adjustments.

5. Nationalism as a consequence of the disruption of social classes engendered by industrialism

The fifth type of explanation specifies some links between the social disorganization caused by industrialization on the one hand and the growth of nationalism on the other. For Eric Kierans, the upheaval in Quebec is due to the sudden opening of a closed and protected society which resulted in a vacuum of leadership, soon filled by extremists; for Ronald Cohen, the explosion of social classes brought about a search for a new identity and for equality; for Peter Desbarats, industrialization created a new proletariat and new elites, the demands of which threatened English Canada as well as the Canadian Confedera-tion; and for E. M. Corbett, the growth of French-Canadian nationalism was attributable to the new middle classes engen-dered by industrialization. The "middle-class theory of French Canadian nationalism," in particular, has been a very popular explanation especially among analysts such as Phillipe Garigue, Raymond Breton, Albert Breton and Pierre Trudeau who considered nationalism as counter-revolutionary.

6. Nationalism as the thirst for material goods engendered by industrialism

The sixth link between industrialization and French-Canadian nationalism goes something like the following: "It's precisely the booming economic progress which is the source of rising intensity between English Canadians and French Canadians" (Norman Smith, 60). Before industrialization, French Canadians with their Roman Catholic values focused largely on non-material aims, and did not experience the cultural coalescing of Protestant dogma and commercial values of industrialism and capitalism.[9] Now, they have tasted the fruits of materialism and found them more and more to their liking, hence, they are asking for more and more of them. Theirs is a case of rising expectations frustrated because the offer could not satisfy a sudden, general and pressing demand; hence nationalism.

7. Nationalism as economic decolonization accentuated by industrialization

According to this thesis, industrialization breeds nationalism in Quebec not so much because of the demand for material goods (which could always be satisfied through the market or through some kind of state intervention) but because of the demand for goods produced and marketed in French and by French Canadians. French Canadians "now want material progress in French" (Eugene Forsey). "Modernization has intensified the impression of outside domination," (Stephen Clarkson), and French Canadians react because they are finding out that "industrialization was carried on largely by English Canadian and American capital" (Janet Morchain). They realize that "the industrial frontier between English Canada and French Canada is still drawn at Cantonville," as Keyfitz said, and resent what they perceive to be economic discrimination by English Canadians and Americans.

8. *Anti-competitive nationalism spurred by industrialization*

Here, industrialization breeds not only a nationalism directed against English Canadians and Americans but also against the basic competitive norms of the economic system of production which is seen as controlled by and biased for English Canadians and Americans. Industrialization creates economic situations where competition turns into quasi-monopoly, thus sharpening nationalism. One example of this phenomenon is that in the new industrial structure the market is seen as becoming less open for new business, hence for potential French-Canadian business. In this structure, also, brainwork becomes highly valued. Since brainwork is closely related to the language one speaks and since the English language is considered necessary for efficient brainwork in most companies, French Canadians feel discriminated against as far as the availability of top jobs is concerned and thus cease to (or fail to begin to) believe in the "equality of opportunity" ethos which is supposed to permeate political and economic affairs in the Western world. Consequently, having found that their individual talents and capacities are not recognized, they turn toward collective aims and ways of thinking: that is, French-Canadian nationalism.

9. *Nationalism based on technological alienation*

The nationalism of some French-Canadian intellectuals is spurred by technology itself and by the perception which they have of the close relationship between technology and Americanization. Their "struggle with the U.S.A.," writes Frank Wilson, "is also moral." It implies a stand "against technicity *à l'américaine*," technological alienation and the "corporate and technological oppression" which leads to "technological uniformity, quantity and inhumanity" and to an "undemocratic rejection of the values of human dignity."[10] These intellectuals interweave nationalism with an anti-technological alienation struggle. Caloren describes this phenomenon as "an alliance between anti-technological imperialism forces and an ethnic collectivity based on language, a compact force of minority against homogenization."

10. *Socialist nationalism*

Finally, socialism and nationalism are often linked together in contemporary Quebec as an indirect result of industrialism. Whereas it is true, in Quebec as elsewhere, that various forms of socialism were born and grew up as a consequence of industrial development, it is also true, as Porter has remarked, that "French Canada could well be described as one of those societies in which class conflict becomes diverted into ethnic hostility." Such a diversion is explained, in part, by the fact that industrialization has given a progressive content to French-Canadian nationalism—as the anti-competitive and the decolonization types of nationalism clearly show—thus rendering possible a tactical collaboration between socialists and the left-oriented new bourgeoisie nationalists who are regarded by the former as a dangerous, but necessary, element of an upcoming revolution. Albert Breton thinks that the alliance between nationalists and socialists has occurred because industrialization has given both the workers and the middle class a common enemy: the old Quebec middle class which is in great part English speaking.

These ten types of positive links between nationalism and industrialization are by no means exhaustive, nor are they mutually exclusive, since they are often used in an interwoven fashion. As types, however, they represent a valid review of the main explanations put forward by the analysts who have tried to account for the emergence of a new form of French-Canadian nationalism in the last decade.

THE PARTI QUÉBÉCOIS PROGRAM AS TECHNOLOGICAL NATIONALISM

We will now attempt to analyse the ideology of today's foremost Quebec nationalist organization, the Parti Québécois, with regard to the types of explanation which we have just identified. Our analysis will be based only upon documents produced by the P.Q. before April 1973, such as its Program, its Executive *Manifesto* and other publications. We will thus be concerned solely with the official attitudes expressed by the P.Q. itself toward industrialism and technology, and not with the general relationship between the P.Q. brand of nationalism and industrialism. In particular, we will not deal with the opinions of any of its leaders on the subject, nor with any factual data (such as the social class of the membership) which might negate or validate some of the explanations identified above.

Survival and Salvation: The Best Chance through Technology

The 1971 P.Q. Program begins with the following lines, which are at the very heart of the present discussion:

Le Québec économique devra entrer dans un monde aux prises avec une révolution permanente du côté des sciences et de la technologie. . . . C'est à ce monde-là, celui d'une explosion sans précédent des connaissances et de leurs applications, qu'il va falloir s'adapter; ce qui est vrai en tout état de cause et sous n'importe quel régime. Mais nous croyons, nous, que c'est par la souveraineté politique que le Québec aura, de loin, le plus de chance de s'en tirer avec honneur—et sa seule chance, modeste mais bien réelle, d'y arriver d'une façon qui soit suffisamment originale pour que sa culture en soit vivifiée et "rentabilisée" au contact de la vie économique, au lieu d'être anémiée comme c'est le cas présentement (P, 5)[11]

We see that the P.Q. Program rests on the premise that the industrial and technological revolution is seen as having had, up until now, an alienating effect on the Quebec culture. Quebec will have to adapt itself to this revolution and political sovereignty is its best chance to adapt in a profitable fashion from the point of view of its culture.

Furthermore, continues the Program, Quebec will soon be engaged in a post-industrial societal development where industrial production will have more and more effect on the cultural behaviour of people. At this stage, the only nations which will remain collective masters of their own destinies will be those who will have succeeded in digesting such phenomena as concentration, inter-penetration and inter-dependence (P, 5).

For the P.Q., then, industrial development poses a clear problem of survival for the French-Canadian culture. The only solution to this problem is a change of attitude toward industrialism and technology. Instead of trying to control the culturally damaging effects of modern economic development by isolating part of its social life into the rural setting as was done in the past, the people of Quebec should now seek to establish control directly over the forces of industrialization. Furthermore, since modern development is global in scope, the solution also has to be global and imply nothing less than the control of all the essential levers of cultural and economic expansion (P, 20; M, 13, 20).

The main lever upon which control has to be established is the state. A unitary state is necessary to put order into the chaos of a regime created at a time when it was impossible to foresee the scientific and technological revolution which now sweeps the whole of Quebec.

"We [i.e., French Canadians] have," says the *Manifesto*, "collectively missed the historical moment when all nations have understood that the rationality and strength of governments were at the very source of economic developments" (M, 56). "It will never be possible to reconstruct Quebec's economy with the actual weak provincial government . . ." (M, 103), and time is pressing: "We need a full national existence which will provide us with the means to face threatening deadlines and this before too many years" (M, 20).

The need for a unitary state as a responsive tool to deal properly with the industrial and technological challenge of our time is one of the most constant themes upon which the P.Q. has insisted since its foundation. The problem then becomes: which state should it be? Ottawa or Quebec? Industrialization and technological developments are thus depicted as the important reasons why the choice has become, in the last years, so drastically dichotomized for French Canadians.

This line of reasoning is especially clear in matters related to education and research. "The technological and cultural revolutions have created economic and social conditions in which education and research have become the true driving force of economic expansion . . . and a guarantee of the autonomy and even the survival of any society" (P, 20). Quebec needs more technical education programs and more technological research. Among others, it faces two obstacles in this sector. First, the federal research policies are detrimental to Quebec (M, 114; *Les dossiers*, 53-69); and secondly, a good portion of the technically competent personnel educated in Quebec have trouble finding jobs corresponding to their capacities, even though everybody agrees that there is a shortage of such technicians in Quebec (M, 64).

Similarly, Quebec needs to make a major effort in research applied to agriculture, not only because technology has given this traditionally family-bound activity all the characteristics of a true industry, but because technology has forced the federal government to intervene on a large scale into this sector of the economy also, often to the detriment of Quebeckers whose interests are not always in line with the Canadian ones (*L'agriculture chez nous*; *Les dossiers*; P, 12, 227-46).

Likewise, with regard to the planning of the economy, the Quebec government's attempts at planning in the mid-sixties were unsuccessful, partly because the actions of both levels of government were at odds. For example, according to the P.Q., Quebec tried to channel its financial help mainly toward industries that were in need of technological modernizations, whereas Ottawa allocated its resources to just about any type of industry, provided it would create jobs (M, 102).

For the P.Q., then, technological development creates a dangerous situation for French Canadians in Quebec because it gives rise to an overall need for organization and control, a function which the federal government is bound to exercise more and more to the disadvantage of Quebeckers. The P.Q., however, does not reject technology as such. On the contrary, it accepts as valid the proposition that technological development is here to stay but must be controlled so as not to produce chaos. It also accepts the idea that proper technological development necessitates centralized control and planning. That is why it wants to transfer all powers to the Quebec government. Once this is done and such powers are firmly and lucidly applied, the P.Q. thinks that nearly miraculous changes can take place and a great number of obstacles which now appear to be insurmountable will then become mere technical problems, easily solvable.

The P.Q. considers, furthermore, that one of the important trumps in the hands of the Quebeckers is the fact that they are relatively familiar with American technological know-how, a familiarity which could be exploited to their advantage instead of passively allowing it to be submerged, as is the case under present conditions. Even the lags of technological developments could become an advantage to the people of Quebec since, in a world of fast-changing economic life engendered by technology, it is often better to create new types of productive systems from scratch, rather than patch up battered ones.

Technology and Foreign Property

We have already noted that the P.Q. views industrial and technological growth as engendering chaos in Quebec because the channels through which such growth should be controlled are split between two levels of government whose actions are seen as mutually disruptive or not properly attuned to the specific needs of Quebeckers. The P.Q. Program offers a global solution to end the chaos: the institution of a single government apparatus with all the powers to initiate and develop orderly growth.

The sources of chaos, however, are not seen as residing in the government itself, but rather in the economic organizations which produce and distribute the goods. These enterprises offer a general characteristic in Quebec: they are under foreign control, leaving the people of Quebec with very little to decide in vast sectors of the economy (P, 7; *Qui contrôle?*, 24, 28). Consequently, the general economic development of Quebec is under foreign control, even though the necessary investment capital comes in great part from local sources (*Qui contrôle?*, 38-43). What is significant, however, is that the situation is deteriorating every day because industrial and technological developments are highly correlated with the general tendency toward economic concentration, interpenetration and interdependence. This tendency also affects the whole of Canada but, as the *Manifesto* says, "that Canada itself is on the verge of becoming an appendix of the American economic empire indicates that Quebec is slipping farther and farther away from the true centres of decision" (M, 20). Even worse, local businessmen and industrialists cannot cope with the foreign industrial empires and thus, instead of making the effort to modernize their enterprises, lay in wait for foreign buyers and a sunny retirement to the Southern part of the hemisphere.

To deal with this situation, the P.Q. proposes a "code of foreign investments" according to which (a) all companies doing business in Quebec would have to be incorporated in Quebec; (b) no company incorporated in Quebec could be 100 per cent foreign-owned; (c) companies dealing with cultural affairs (mass media, printed matters), and raw steel would have to be 100 per cent locally owned; and (d) bank trusts, insurance, railroad, electric and communication products companies could not be more than 49 per cent foreign-owned (M, 93-100).

It is interesting to note that among the few exceptions to the above rules, the P.Q. would consider it admissible to permit majority foreign ownership in the case of companies which operate in new technological fields because "it is often less costly to accept such control than to face the high costs of royalties on new patents" (M, 100).

Technology and Anti-competitiveness

The need for control which the P.Q. sees as rising from the spread of industrialization and technology is very relevant to the notion of competitiveness. It is obvious that under a P.Q. government, the state would vastly expand its economic activities. The program is explicit on this point:

Modern states can implement their policies either by creating their own instruments or by multiplying controls applicable to private enterprises. This second formula has already demonstrated its serious shortcomings in as much as companies systematically try to avoid the controls which consequently become more numerous and bureaucratized. Given these conditions, the efficiency of a state's actions depends on the instruments it has given itself in order to accelerate industrialization and technological development . . . this formula includes certain nationalizations . . . and especially the creation of new enterprises, of government financial reserves and management bodies. Consequently, the state shall adopt as a primary form of economic intervention, a sustained extension of the public sector (state or mixed enterprises) (P, 7).

As a corollary to state expansion, the P.Q. strongly believes in efficient state planning. A péquiste government would establish a planning office whose central economic objective would be the modernization and up-dating of Quebec's economy.

There are two main reasons why the P.Q. rejects the liberal concept of free competition as a basic economic philosophy. First, it claims that the scientific and technological revolutions have brought about an irreversible trend of industrial concencentration which in fact has done away with competitiveness or created a "faked" one in many economic sectors. In such a context, it becomes more important for the state to help develop large enterprises and fight "abusive fractioning of markets" (M, 96) than to try restoring free competition. On the other hand, the *Manifesto* recognizes that the advent of technology has contributed to a sharpening of international economic competition which is unavoidable. To meet this competition, the Quebec economy—largely dependent on exports—cannot rely on chaotic internal competition; hence state intervention (M, 53-54).

Secondly, the P.Q. refutes the philosophical premise underlying the competitive spirit, which is the belief that individuals are wolf-like and society is but a jungle whose best chance of progress lies in the fierce confrontation of instincts and appetites. It regards this view as a "false individual freedom" which becomes the privilege of the fox in the hen-house, the strong over the weak and the big over the small (M, 36-37). Furthermore, it considers that the growth of industrialization and technology has given rise to a kind of anarchic neo-individualism whose baneful consequences are worse than ever, if one considers the present lack of economic democracy, the unjust sharing of products and resources and the vulnerability of consumers.

Participatory Democracy versus the Ills of Technology and Technocracy

While the P.Q. is generally favourable to bigness in government and enterprises, it is also very conscious of the dangers involved in such a formula: industrialization and technology are inexorably pushing societies toward bigness which, in turn, breeds inhuman bureaucracies, technostructures, alienation of the workers in the enterprises, a pervasive conflictual situation between man and the economic structures and consequently an overall danger for civilization.

The most important aims of the P.Q. Program in human terms are the humanization of the internal rhythm brought about by the scientific and technological revolution, the fulfillment of human capacities and dignity of all individuals, and the subordination of economic affairs to individual and societal needs (P, 15, 18; M, 35, 56, 104).

Both the political and the economic structures will have to be profoundly modified so as to meet these aims and to avoid the pitfalls of technology. Concerning the government, it is proposed that all efforts should be made to organize the participation of citizens in the over-all decision-making process and even in the day-to-day administration of public affairs. Such participation would be insured by an extensive and decentralized planning agency, a deconcentration of government services to regional and local levels and the institution of new forms of management (auto-management and co-management) in such sectors as municipal affairs and education.

As for enterprises, although the P.Q. clearly favours their regrouping into large units, it nevertheless considers that they will also have to submit to new managerial formats in order to permit the "re-entry of men into the productive apparatus" (M, 70, 125) through participation. In this regard, its proposals are many-fold: a) workers' unions would be created in all enterprises; b) in all public enterprises and in major private ones, workers' representatives would sit on the governing bodies; c) cooperative organizations would be formally and financially supported by the state in such sectors as savings, loans, insurances, agriculture, mass media, editing, films and taxis; and d) total management by the workers in lumbering and by the citizens in public housing would be instituted.

Quantity or Quality?

We have seen that some authors attribute the contemporary rise in French-Canadian nationalism to a change of attitude toward material goods. The P.Q. Program relates in part to this hypothesis. It proposes the development of economic production as an official policy, but it also says that such objectives will have to be reconciled with the construction of a participatory society. Furthermore, it expresses concern over the many "thorny problems and contagious dissatisfactions produced by the type of existence which technology, automation and publicity have imposed upon mankind" (M, 47). Consumer protection laws, publicity control, early retirement and vigorous cultural and recreational policies are among the P.Q. measures which could enhance the quality of life. The P.Q. *Manifesto* is also alert to the counter-productivity engendered by technologically-based economic growth: artificial and potentially dangerous products, environmental problems, and so on. When all has been considered, however, the P.Q. remains hopeful that technological progress and economic expansion will not prove to be in opposition to cultural development in as much as they permit the physical liberation of the workers, thus giving them access to cultural goods.

Conclusion: The Evolution of Technological Nationalism

Some analysts have evoked a ghastly nightmare concerning the evolution of nationalism in Quebec; according to them, the systematic belief in the use of technology in fulfilment of nationalistic aims could bring about a rightist form of government which would seriously endanger democracy in Quebec. Our analysis of the official P.Q. documents gives no indication that such prospective developments are in the making.

First, its ideology is not totalitarian, either in aims or in means. Because it thinks that the ever-expanding changes in the mode of production and distribution of goods have created a chaotic situation which is potentially dangerous for Quebec society, its whole program, including political sovereignty for Quebec, is presented as a response to the challenges of our times. It insists very much, however, that such a response be orderly, that is through elections, and progressive without falling prey to any doctrinaire ideologies.

"We are searching for a new order," says the *Manifesto*, "but we will not try to jump over normal stages. In particular, we refuse to participate in dialectic pettifoggeries in which independence is classified as a petit bourgeois objective, government modernization as a form of state capitalism and social revolution as a modern-type petty leftism. Such oppositions would divide and reduce us to such powerlessness that they are the objective basis of the status quo" (M, 36-37). If the P.Q. rejects doctrinaire socialism, it also finds "capitalism à la grand-papa" utterly unacceptable (M, 129). It intends to be judged by its policies toward the multitude of unorganized and unprovided-for: workers, old people, children and the handicapped.

It must be said, however, that in recent years, the P.Q. has drastically dampened its commitment to technological nationalism. The 1973 edition of its program—which was prepared by the Executive Committee and published prior to the October 1973 elections—is more electoral in content, and emphasizes specific problems and solutions without much reference to social philosophical stands and sweeping socio-economic analysis. In particular, the new program omits the prior P.Q. theory according to which the magnitude and swiftness of the social changes brought about by the advent of technological industrialization imparted urgency on the realization of Quebec's independence. Likewise, it barely deals with the general problems of technological bigness like those of power concentration, work dehumanization and bureaucratic inflation and it remains absolutely mute on such contemporary socio-technological issues as energy, transport and urban development. Finally, it now appears that the P.Q. is more intent on establishing the means of political and commercial control over technology and industrialization than on defining the aims towards which these tools should be put to use.

BIBLIOGRAPHY

BOOKS AND ARTICLES

Breton, Albert, "The Economics of Nationalism," *Journal of Political Economy* (August 1964), pp. 376-86.
Breton, Raymond and André Breton, "Le Séparatisme ou le respect du statu quo," *Cité Libre* (Avril 1962), pp. 17-18.

Caloren, Fred, "Nationalism in Quebec, 1967," *Christian Century,* July 1968, pp. 913-29; also in W. E. Mann, ed., *Canada: A Sociological Profile* (Toronto: Copp Clark, 1968) , pp. 498-506.

Clark, Gerald, *Canada: The Uneasy Neighbor* (Toronto: McClelland and Stewart, 1965).

Clarkson, Stephen, "A Programme for Binational Development," in Peter Russell, ed., *Nationalism in Canada* (Toronto: McGraw-Hill, 1966), pp. 133-52.

Cohen, Ronald, *Le Vote au Québec; les "pourquoi" et "comment" du vote fédéral au Québec depuis la Conféderation* (Montréal: Sage Production, 1965).

Cook, Ramsay, *Canada and the French-Canadian Question* (Toronto: Macmillan, 1966).

Corbett, E. M., *Quebec Confronts Canada* (Baltimore: John Hopkins University Press, 1967) .

Corry, James A., "Constitutional Trends and Federalism," in Paul Fox, ed., *Politics: Canada, Recent Readings* (Toronto: McGraw-Hill, 1962), pp. 26-40.

Craig, Gerald M., *The United States and Canada* (Cambridge, Mass.: Harvard University Press, 1968).

De Roussan, Jacques, *Les Canadiens et nous* (Montréal: Editions de l'homme, 1964) .

Desbarats, Peter, *The State of Quebec: A Journalist's View of the Quiet Revolution* (Toronto: McClelland and Stewart, 1964).

Forsey, Eugene, "Concepts of Federalism: Some Canadian Aspects," in Gordon Hawkins, ed., *Concepts of Federalism* (Toronto: Canadian Institute on Public Affairs, 1965), pp. 22-29.

Garigue, Philippe, *L'Option politique du Canada français* (Montréal: Editions du Levrier, 1963) .

Kelly, George A., "French Canada's New Left," *Orbis,* Vol. IX, No. 2 (Summer 1965), pp. 393-410.

Keyfitz, Nathan, "Canadians and Canadians," *Queen's Quarterly,* Vol. LXX, No. 2 (Summer 1963), pp. 163-82.

——, "French Canada Still in Transition," Foreword to the new edition of Everett C. Hughes' *French Canada in Transition* (Toronto: University of Toronto Press, 1963), pp. v-vii.

Kierans, Eric, *Le Canada vu par Kierans* (Montréal: Editions du Jour, 1967), a translation of *Challenge of Confidence: Kierans on Canada* (Toronto: McClelland and Stewart, 1967).

McRae, Kenneth D., "The Structure of Canadian History," in Louis Hartz, ed., *The Founding of New Societies* (New York: Harcourt, 1964), pp. 219-74.

Morchain, Janet Kerr, *Search for a Nation: French English Relations in Canada since 1759* (Toronto: Dent, 1967) .

Myers, Hugh Binghan, *The Quebec Revolution* (Montreal: Harvest House, 1964).

Pearson, L. B. "Changing Canadian Federalism," in J. Peter Meekison, ed., *Canadian Federalism: Myth or Reality* (Toronto: Methuen, 1968), pp. 406-12.

Porter, John, *The Vertical Mosaic* (Toronto: University of Toronto Press, 1968).

Rotstein, Abraham, "The 20th Century Prospect: Nationalism in a Technological Society," in Peter Russell, ed., *Nationalism in Canada* (Toronto: McGraw-Hill, 1966), pp. 341-63.

Russell, Peter, "Conclusion," in *Nationalism in Canada*, pp. 364-77.

Sloan, Thomas, "New Technology in French Canada," *Montreal Star* (March 1, 1966), p. 6.

Smith, J. Norman, "The Canadian Sense of Destiny," in Livingston T. Merchant, ed., *Neighbors Taken for Granted* (New York: Praeger, 1966), pp. 34-62.

Trudeau, P. E., "La nouvelle trahison des clerc," 29 *Cité Libre* (Avril 1962), pp. 3-16.

Wilson, Edmund, *O Canada, An American's Notes on Canadian Culture* (New York: Farrar, Strauss and Giroux, 1964).

Wilson, Frank L., "French Canadian Separatism," *Western Political Quarterly*, Vol. XX (March 1967), pp. 116-31.

PUBLICATIONS OF THE PARTI QUÉBÉCOIS

(All published by Les Editions du Parti Québécois)

Comment se fera l'indépendance (1972)

L'Agriculture chez nous (1972)

Le Programme du Parti Québécois (1972)

Les Dossiers du quatrième congrès national du Parti Québécois (1972)

Quand nous serons vraiment chez nous (1972)

Qui contrôle l'économie du Québec? (1972)

Témoignage de Camille Laurin (1971)

Le Programme (1971)

Le Programme (1973)

NOTES

1. George A. Kelly, "French Canada's New Left," pp. 394-95. (Complete bibliographical details of works cited in this essay will be found on pages 165-67).

2. James A. Corry, "Constitutional Trends and Federalism," p. 12.

3. John Porter, *The Vertical Mosaic*, p. 383.

4. Norman J. Smith, "The Canadian Sense of Destiny," p. 60.

5. Lester B. Pearson, "Changing Canadian Federalism," p. 408.

6. Jacques de Roussan, *Les Canadiens et nous*, pp. 23-25.

7. Nathan Keyfitz, "Canadians and Canadiens," p. 175.

8. Edmund Wilson, *O Canada, An American's Notes on Canadian Culture*,

p. 12; and Kenneth McRae, "The Structure of Canadian History," p. 271.

9. Smith, "Canadian Sense of Destiny," p. 60; and Porter, *Vertical Mosaic*, p. 95.

10. Kelly, "French Canada's New Left," pp. 401, 410; and Fred Caloren, "Nationalism in Quebec, 1967," p. 505.

11. Hereafter, quotations will refer to the Program (P), the *Manifesto* (M) and to other P.Q. publications (specifically identified). The number refers to the page from which the quotation is taken. Translations are mine.

Contributors

HOWARD ASTOR teaches Political Science at McMaster University. He received his B.A. from McGill, and pursued his doctoral work at Yale and the London School of Economics. In addition to writing on Canadian politics and political philosophy, he is an editor at Mosaic Press.

STEPHEN CLARKSON has written extensively on Canada and Canadian foreign policy. He teaches Politics at the University of Toronto, and is the editor of *An Independent Foreign Policy for Canada?*

EDOUARD CLOUTIER attended the University of Montreal and received his doctorate in Political Science from the University of Rochester. He was one of the first vice-presidents of the *Rassemblement pour l'independence Nationale.* He now teaches at the University of Montreal.

WALLACE GAGNE, a native of Vancouver, received his doctorate in Political Science from the University of Rochester. He is presently living in Calgary, where he works as a freelance writer and commentator.

PAUL PHILLIPS has written numerous articles on Canadian labour. He is the author of *No Power Greater,* a history of the Canadian labour movement. He teaches Economics at the University of Manitoba.

JOHN WOODS is a native of Winnipeg. He attended the University of Manitoba and received his doctorate in Political Science from Stanford. He teaches Political Science at the University of Calgary.